A Father
A Son
and A House
Full of Ghosts

Gregory Young

Copyright © 2006 by Gregory Young

ISBN 0-7414-3536-5

Published by:

INFI∞ITY
PUBLISHING.COM

1094 New DeHaven Street, Suite 100
West Conshohocken, PA 19428-2713
Info@buybooksontheweb.com
www.buybooksontheweb.com
Toll-free (877) BUY BOOK
Local Phone (610) 941-9999
Fax (610) 941-9959

Printed in the United States of America

Printed on Recycled Paper

Published December 2006

This book is dedicated to
Elizabeth Agnes Jensen
(1820-1898)

*For if it had not been for her,
there would have been no story to tell.*

Special Thanks to:

Sharon Dvorak, Judith DeBrosse, Catherine La Drew, Lou Ann Rest, Joseph Young and friends of Lower Township.

And to Those in Spirit:

Agnes, Jonathan, Sarah, Ma-Ryah, John

CONTENTS

The Following is a True Story.

1.

I Must Be Crazy

I needed some answers. The unexplainable occurrences in this house were happening more and more frequently. I couldn't go on living like this. No matter where I was, I would be thinking about it. I couldn't get it out of my mind. None of it made sense.

I was searching for someone simply just to listen and to understand but I couldn't find anyone. I would tell these stories to people and they would look at me like I was crazy. They thought something was wrong with me. I began to think it myself. Was I losing my mind? Was this all in my head? Or, was I going through something extraordinary, something so rare and unbelievable that there just isn't anyone to talk about it with. I was becoming more and more confused. I constantly thought about it and I never knew what was going to happen next or when.

The stories were adding up. There was certainly something in this house. There had to be. Both my ten year old son and I were becoming increasingly convinced.

This is nothing that I would have ever wanted to expose him to, but he was here a lot of the times when these strange occurrences occurred. He witnessed them too. He could see the fear in my face and hear the panic in my voice. He and I would talk about it and try to come up with explanations, but just couldn't.

It was the simple things. Things like losing power to the kitchen overhead light. This light would go off for hours or even days at a time and then suddenly would come back on again under its own recognizance. And, once it went off, I had no control over it. It turned into a dead switch. There wasn't anything that I could do. It did what it pleased.

Maybe if I hadn't had the entire kitchen completely rewired a year ago it might have made more sense, but the work was done by professional electricians who brought the entire kitchen up to code with all new outlets, new lights, new circuit breakers, panel box and new meters on the outside of the house. The light would simply go out on its own, at random whenever I would be in the kitchen.

It was the same with the tall touch light on the long sideboard table in the dining room. This light also had a mind of its own. I would turn it off and minutes later I would turn to see it back on again. I would again turn it off, and it would again come back on. This would go on and on until I simply just left it alone and let it do what it wanted. Then, the next night the light would behave just as a lamp should. It went on when I turned it on and would go off when I turned it off. Days later it would go crazy, off, on, off, on, off, on. I could not compete with these lights, nor did I have an explanation.

I also had no explanation as to how I could set my keys on the kitchen counter only to come back moments later to find them completely gone. I searched the counter frantically, knowing that I had just put them in that spot minutes ago. Then after searching the floor and the surrounding area, I walk into another room for a moment, and when I return back in the kitchen, I find the keys back on the kitchen counter exactly in the original spot where I knew that I had left them.

My son Joey and I also couldn't explain why the CD player which sits on top of the refrigerator in the kitchen went on by itself at 7:30 A.M. on a Saturday morning. It went on completely on its own blasting the CD that was left in there. We were still in bed but were woken up to track twelve of Green Day's American Idiot CD blasting throughout the house. Today, the CD player will only play fifteen seconds of that song and then will go completely silent.

With the many strange occurrences that have happened in this house, I don't remember a time when either one of us were truly scared. It was more a case of being shocked, shocked at what we saw or what had happened. I didn't have any answers, but I had a lot of questions, and the most formidable question was, is there something living in this house with us?

2.

A Handyman's Special

It started in September of the year 2000. Winter was approaching quickly and I needed to buy a house before the cold weather set in.

My living conditions at the time were unsuitable for myself and my five year old son. We were living in a small room underneath a garage where there was no kitchen and no bath or shower. Showers had to be taken outside and meals were cooked in either the microwave or on an electric hot plate. Most of the time, we simply ordered out. My son at that time was five years old and staying with me two nights a week. But, it was still very embarrassing to have to explain to him that these had to be our living conditions at this time until a house in our price range came along. The cost to live there was close to nothing and it allowed me to save money for a down payment for a house in a short amount of time.

My real estate agent was beginning to feel my desperation also. Every night he would check the internet for any new listings. We both knew that we were going to have to act quickly if something came up. Houses were moving fast in this shore town and you had to be ready to move quickly if something new was on the market.

The real estate market at that time was very competitive. Sellers were getting offers beyond the asking price, and houses were lasting only days after being listed.

I remember getting the phone call from my agent around 8:00 one morning. He made me aware that a house had just gone on the market the night before. There was no sale sign on it yet and it would take a couple of days before it would be printed in the real estate MLS book. I excitedly got dressed as we agreed to meet at the property in an hour.

The street that this house was located on, I had driven down many times before but had never noticed this house. It sat back off the road, much more than the other houses on the residential street, and it had two very large over grown trees blocking it from anyone passing by. If you didn't know the house was there, then you wouldn't know that it was there. In fact, if my agents white pick up truck hadn't been parked on the curb outside of the property, I would have driven right past it.

He had only been waiting a minute or two when I pulled up in my car. We both got out of our vehicles as the same time.

We knew that no one would be home. He had called the real estate office as soon as they had opened to make the arrangements to pick up the key. We walked into the front door to find a dilapidating outdated house with low ceilings, an old carpet smelling of dirt and must, dirty paneled walls and slanted floors. The kitchen was functional but unattractive and outdated. There was a fuse box for electricity and the old oil furnace was on its last legs. The old wooden joists in the basement were being held up with jack posts and there was termite damage throughout. The house, as we later learned was built in the year 1904 and at this time, was ninety-six years old.

The most positive aspect of this house however, was the location. The location was fantastic. It was in walking distance to a shopping complex, a sports complex, night clubs, the bay, a hospital, and one short trip over the bridge and you're in a million dollar town called Ocean City.

Other positive aspects included a garage, a shed, a private backyard, and inside the house was a charming banister which lead to the second floor.

As we walked up these steps to the second floor, we noticed a small landing at the top with only two bedrooms. After jumping up and down on the floor it seemed that the upstairs was structurally unstable. The floors bounced like a WWF wrestling ring. In short, the house was a mess and I knew that the projects would be endless in trying to improve it.

It was the location though that sold me. That and the private backyard. It was just big enough to throw a football for a catch-perfect for my son and I.

After fifteen minutes of going through the house and walking around the property, I told my agent that I was interested enough to present an offer. The price was right. I figured that I would worry about all of that structural damage stuff later. Just get me into this house as soon as possible. I can't stand living in that small room underneath the garage anymore.

Shortly after, that same day, he drew up the papers and we presented an offer. The house listed for $80,000 and we offered $78,000. They took it. The papers were signed and the house was now under agreement with my name on the contract as the buyer.

The next day we learned that five other phone calls had come into the sellers real estate office from potential buyers interested in the property. Fortunately for me, the papers had already been signed and the house was mine unless I decided to back out of the deal.

The agreement now, after being signed, goes through a three day attorney review process in which the buyer has the right to withdraw their offer for any reason if they so desire. Just to make sure I was doing the right thing, I figured that I should probably visit the house once more before the three day attorney review was over. After all, I had decided to buy this house only after fifteen minutes of looking at it.

When we went back to take our second look, it again became obvious that the fix up projects would be endless. And there was something else that was in the house which was not there the first time. This time, the owner was home.

She had greeted us at the door and my agent immediately apologized for the confusion and missed communication. "We weren't aware that anyone would be home," he said.

"It's all right," said the woman. "Come in."

She was pleasant and was eager to talk. She was an eighty-two year old woman who had been a widow for twelve years. She explained that she can no longer keep up with the high maintenance of the house. She and her husband had owned the house for thirty-nine years, keeping it mostly as their summer home while they would visit from Pennsylvania. It was in the last twelve years though, after her husband had died, that she decided to live there permanently.

This pleasant older woman's name was Evelyn, and as lively as she was in still wanting to go out with the girls and play cards, she was older and her health would not allow her to go on without additional care. She planned to move into an assisted living retirement home located in Ocean City-the town just over the bridge.

Evelyn was very friendly. We stood in the kitchen and talked, and she invited me to sit down at the kitchen table. "My husband loved to go fishing," she told me. "He loved this place...oh, and the parties we would have. I have so many memories here. I hate to leave, but it needs so much work and my health isn't what it used to be," she explained. "By the way," she asked. "What would a man like you want with an old house like this?"

"I've always liked older houses." I said.

7

"Oh," she said with a look of surprise.

From that point on, Evelyn referred to me as the gentleman who likes older houses.

After leaving the house from my second visit, I had a very warm feeling. There was no question in my mind now that this was it. Buying this house was the right thing to do. I knew that I had made the right decision. I remember saying to myself, I don't care what's wrong with it or how much work it needs. I'll just take it one day at a time and work on it. I'll try to bring it back to life.

My visit today convinced me that this house had a warm history to it. It had been very important to the people living here, for it held thirty-nine years of their memories. As dilapidating as it may have appeared to the buyer, it was clear that it had a wonderful past, and with some care and a lot of work it still had a chance for a future.

3.

The Sense of a Presence

After a couple of years working on it and completing projects, the house really started to take shape. I converted the heat from oil to gas. I converted the electric from fuses to circuit breakers. And I undertook the first major project of the house. I gutted the entire kitchen down to studs and started over. I had the kitchen rewired by professional electricians who brought it up to code. New lighting was installed, a new sanded hardwood floor and new up-to-date plumbing and appliances.

Month after month, project after project, I went from room to room and worked on this old house. It was also at this time that I began a new relationship with a woman named Nancy. We dated for a few months until she decided to rent out her condo and to move into the house with me. The times were happy. We were both enjoying this small cozy house and the company of each other. And after twelve short months we were engaged to be married.

Nancy and I married in November of 2002 and continued to live there. There were still many projects to be undertaken but Nancy seemed to be tolerant of it. Suddenly though, it seemed that the size of the house started to get to her. She started to complain that the house was too small and that we should sell it and move. I was very surprised to hear this because she so often commented on how much she loved the house. She often told me that she was very happy living here. Then one day she decides that she doesn't want to live here anymore.

Unbeknownst to me at that time, something else was making her unhappy. Nancy sensed something. She sensed a presence in the house. The first time that I had heard of it was when she called it to my attention one afternoon as she came up the stairs from the basement. She had just come up from the old basement after doing a load of wash. I don't know what happened down there. I only remember her walking up the basement stairs which led into the dining room. She had her hands full with folded towels. Her face was very serious, and it was obvious that something was bothering her. I asked her what was wrong. She then spoke the following words. She said, "There is something in this house and it doesn't like me."

I stood quietly and watched her walk away into the living room and up the stairs to the second floor. Anything I would have said in response to that would have seemed insensitive and pointless. I kept quiet and remained motionless as she kept walking.

It wasn't long before Nancy and I started to argue over even the smallest of things.

4.

Happy Holidays

Christmas was soon approaching. It was one month after being married and two weeks after her saying, "There is something in this house and it doesn't like me." This was going to be our first Christmas together in this house. We were excited. It was around this time though that three more incidents happened involving Nancy.

The first incident happened during a time when she was gift wrapping. She had a brown paper shopping bag from the supermarket which was filled with Christmas wrapping materials. In the bag were scissors, ribbon, bows, tape, boxes and cards. She folded up the bag and put the bag in the middle of the dining room table in the morning before going to work. Her plan was to wrap presents that evening after getting home from work.

However, when she arrived home from work that evening, the bag was not on the table. There was nothing on the dining room table. She looked all around the dining area. She then looked in both the living room and the kitchen thinking that she was mistaken about where she had left it, but there was no bag. She even went upstairs thinking that she had done something else with it, but there was no bag.

Being the skeptic that I was and knowing that she didn't like the house anyway, the thought did cross my mind that she had made this whole story up to try and convince me that there was a presence in the house and that we should sell it and move somewhere else. I did however become convinced that her story was true after I overheard her making several phone calls to her friends and sister telling them what had happened, how she couldn't explain it, and how disturbed she was by it.

During that same holiday season, a second incident occurred. We had gotten our first Christmas tree together and we decided to put it up that night. The ornaments that I had to decorate with were simply awful. Nancy on the other hand, had a collection of very nice ornaments and we decided to use those to decorate the tree. Her ornaments included: beautiful white lights, red bows, lustrous sparkling angels and glittering stars. The tree was decorated elegantly and was perhaps one of the nicest decorated trees that I have ever been a part of.

After the task of putting up the tree, we decorated it, had some wine to celebrate and then went to bed.

The next morning we awoke to find that during the night the tree had toppled over onto the floor. Not only did the tree fall over but we then discovered that the heads of the angel ornaments had broken off. The angels had become headless. Most of the other ornaments had survived the crash.

Nancy made a much bigger deal out of this than I did. Even though I was surprised, I simply attributed the fall of the tree to the tree not sitting in the stand correctly and somehow it fell over during the night. I took total blame for it. It was me who put the tree in the stand in the first place.

The fact is though, the tree was in the stand the entire time we were decorating it, and it was very stable throughout the process. Nevertheless, I told her that maybe something gave way and the tree simply fell over as Christmas trees sometimes do. I didn't however, have an explanation for the heads of the angels.

The third incident was the worst one for me. It was when Nancy fell down the basement stairs. She was going down to do wash, lost her footing and tumbled down. Even though she was hanging onto the handrail, she managed to fall.

Through the rest of that winter and into the early spring it seemed that Nancy and I were completely at odds with each other. Not only for the reasons above but for other reasons as well. We both became very unhappy, very angry, and very dissatisfied with the relationship.

Towards the end of that summer, Nancy moved out of the house and rented a small house on her own. It wasn't too long after that, we decided to divorce, and so ended the short eighteen month marriage.

5.

What's with the Electric?

Nancy moved into a little house in Ocean City and seemed to be relieved of the burden from this one. We kept in touch for a little while in trying to return personal items to each other that may have gotten put into the wrong boxes, and we communicated once or twice through the mail, but after that both of us realized that a friendship simply wasn't going to work. So much damage had been done. Any conversation we would have would only lead to an argument and finger pointing as to who was to blame. After a short while, all contact had been cut off.

The house now basically sat empty. Nancy had taken all of the living room, dining room and bedroom furniture. She also took all of the curtains, the television and the dishes.

Maybe it was the empty house that got me noticing things more. Maybe it was because I would stand in the middle of an empty living room many nights wondering what I was going to do. Whatever it was, I don't think I started paying attention or noticing strange things myself until after she had left. It seemed like things started to happen which were becoming more and more noticeable.

One thing that kept happening was I kept losing electrical power to the entire house. The electric would shut off for only a second at a time, but it would be enough to darken the lights, throw off all of the digital clocks, and erase the message on the telephone answering machine. There was no apparent reason at all. This frequent occurrence happened

14

in any weather. Very often it happened when there was no rain, no wind, and not a cloud in the sky. It seemed to happen most though during the early morning hours, somewhere between midnight and six o'clock A.M.

Eventually, I decided to spend $900 to have new wiring run from the utility pole across the street to the house. I had all of the main wires checked out and the ones connected to the house were replaced. But even after that, it still continued. At this point, I couldn't explain it. I only had so much time to think about these things. I had a career to tend to and a child to care for. I didn't have a lot of time to sit around and ponder all of the possible explanations as to how this was happening. I simply went on with my daily life, dealing with the problem and ignoring it at the same time.

6.

The Pretzel Puzzle

Within the weeks and months ahead, I had bought some new curtains, had gotten some used furniture from yard sales and flea markets, and I had many talks with my son about what had happened and why Nancy and I had separated. Joey was sad but at the same time, he understood. After some tears and the reminiscing of the good times that we had with her, we agreed that it would be appropriate to start some new good times with just he and I. "We're going to make this house a happy place again," I told him. He agreed that this is what we should be doing. After all, we both really liked this house and I was very relieved that I wasn't going to lose it in a divorce settlement.

It was the fall of the year 2004 now. Nancy left back in August and I used the months of September and October to try and get the house back in order. Joey and I would have a lot of fun during these months. We would watch television together, eat snacks, play hide and seek, play board games, have football catches and talk and talk. In short, I spoiled him. I gave him time, and I gave him my attention. He was spending three nights a week with me now, and I tried to make living here as normal as I possibly could. Everything was going well and after a short while, we set up our own daily routines. It was in early November though when two things happened in the house that I couldn't explain.

One November evening around 7:00 P.M. Joey and I were sitting in the living room watching television. He was sitting on the couch and I was sitting on the winged back yellow chair in the small living room. We weren't too far away from each other. During a commercial break he turned to me and asked if we had any snacks to eat. I told him to go into the kitchen, to look around and let me know what he felt like having. I would get up and make it for him. He got up from the couch and went into the kitchen. I knew that he was looking in the cabinets because I heard the doors close. I also knew that he had been looking in the refrigerator and then the freezer because I heard those doors shut also.

Out of the corner of my eye while still watching the television, I saw that he had a box of something in his hand. It was a box of frozen super pretzels. "Can I have two of these?" he asked.

"Yes," I responded quietly. I hesitated in my response because for the life of me I didn't remember buying them. I even spoke out loud asking myself the question, When did I buy those? "Yes Joey, you can have two of those." He sat back down on the couch and I then got up to go into the kitchen. I read the cooking directions on the back of the box and preheated the oven to the specified 425 degrees. I then got out a baking sheet pan. While opening and unwrapping the pretzels I couldn't help wondering when it was that I put them into my shopping cart. I started to think that I was losing my mind. Maybe somebody accidentally put them in the wrong cart. I shook it off, opened the salt packet, sprinkled the salt on the pretzels and put the tray into the oven.

There were six pretzels to the box. I cooked two of them. I then twisted the bag in which the four remaining pretzels were in and put them back into the box. I then closed the white salt packet and sealed that together with a clothes pin. I remember vividly putting the clothes pin on the salt packet. I know that I did this. I also know that I then put the salt packet into the box making sure that I did not disrupt the clothes pin and end up with salt all over the box. I opened up the freezer and put the box of pretzels on one of the shelves.

Two nights later, Joey and I were again sitting in the

living room with he on the couch and me in the chair when he again asked, "Dad, could I have those pretzels again as a snack?"

"Sure Joey, you liked those didn't you." I said with a smile on my face.

"Yes, he confirmed."

Within a few minutes I got up from the chair, went into the kitchen and preheated the oven to 425 degrees. I reached to the left of the oven to get a baking sheet pan and I set it on the counter. I then opened up the freezer to get the pretzels. My heart started pounding when the realization set in. There were no pretzels in the freezer. There were no pretzels. "I know I put those pretzels in here," I told myself. "Where are they?"

"Dad, are you alright?" Joey called from the living room.

"Joey, have you been in this freezer? Have you seen those pretzels?"

"No," he called out.

"I can't find them." I explained. "I know I put them in here."

"Where could they be?" he asked.

"I don't know."

With that, I pulled everything out of the freezer and put it on the counter. This included the frozen pizza, frozen vegetables, the frozen meats, rolls and ice cream. The freezer was now empty.

It was then that I became a little frantic. My voice was nervous, and I felt the blood disappear from my face. "Joey, where are those pretzels?" I asked him looking for some sort of comfort.

"I don't know. What did you do with them?" he asked.

"I know I put them in here. Let me check the refrigerator."

I then opened up the refrigerator, scanned each shelf and then pulled everything out and laid it on the counter. They weren't in there.

I then lost all logic. I opened all of the kitchen cabinets and looked behind the dishes, glasses and canned goods. I looked in the dishwasher, looked in the lazy Susan, and underneath the sink. I then got a brainstorm to search the trash. I picked through the trash in the kitchen. Not finding any clues, I went to the back alley where most of the weeks trash is held waiting for the trash men. I went through each bag. The search was unsuccessful.

"Dad, what's going on?" Joey asked.

"Those pretzels are missing," I said. "You saw those pretzels right? You ate them. How could they just disappear like that?"

"Dad, this is scary."

Once I saw Joey start to get scared, that was when I tried to gain all of my composure back and laugh it off. The last thing I wanted to do was to upset him. We both walked back into the house from the alley, put everything back into the refrigerator and freezer and then went to watch T.V.

I told him that I was going to stop thinking about it. I tried, but I couldn't. My eyes were watching the T.V. but my mind was racing. Racing with the events that had just happened. Racing to retrace my steps from a couple of nights ago while making those pretzels. And replaying the words that I had spoken to my son which showed my fear. I wasn't sure what I had even said, and I wasn't sure if I would sleep through the night. The only thing that I was absolutely sure of, was the fact that I know I had put those pretzels back in the freezer.

7.

A Table for Eight

Two to three weeks later something else happened. While adding accessories to the kitchen, I had decided to clean out the silverware drawer. I didn't have a lot of silverware. Nancy took most of it. She left a few forks and knives so I would have something to eat with, but it wasn't enough. I decided to go out and buy a setting for eight. I picked out the pattern that I wanted and bought a new white plastic silverware holder that would easily fit into the drawer. I cleaned out the drawer wiping out any dust or crumbs. I laid down a small sheet of shelf paper, slid in the plastic silverware holder and placed all of my new silverware into it.

I was excited to have a setting for eight. This means that I now had the potential to have a small dinner party with eight people. I have the silverware to do it.

Later that night, feeling like I accomplished something, I went to bed, toyed around with a guest list and peacefully went to sleep.

Early the next morning, I got dressed for work and went down to the kitchen. Before I walked out the door, I thought that I would open the silverware drawer to marvel at the success of my task the night before. However, when I pulled the drawer open, there lying on top of the new forks was an old antique sterling silver fork. I was dumbfounded. I stood there and just looked at it. I stared at its shape, its color and I wondered its age. I picked it up and held it in my hand. I knew that I had never seen this before, and I knew that it hadn't been in the drawer the night before.

8.

Dreams

As far as the Christmas tree falling, the bag of wrapping materials missing, the pretzels disappearing, the fork appearing, and the lights going off and on, I'm sure a skeptic would come up with a logical explanation for all of them. There was one such incident though that a skeptic could have difficulty with. It happened when I was having my heating system converted from oil to gas.

Two technicians knocked on my door on a chilly morning. They identified themselves as being from the heating company. They told me they had the new heater in the truck and were here to install it. I was thrilled that they were here as early as they were. I was told that they would be there sometime in the morning. I let them in, showed them the basement and they got to work. They were down there for hours, but I didn't care. I just wanted the job done because at that time I had no heat and the nights were colder than normal average temperatures for the time of year.

I went down to check on them. They seemed to be having a difficult job of getting the new furnace into the small space that was designated for it. With patience and perseverance though, they did it. But, for some reason they couldn't get it working.

I was under the assumption that they would come, hook everything up and in a matter of hours I would have heat, and life would be back to normal again. All hopes were shattered however when one of the technicians came up to talk to me. "Uh...It's unlikely that you will have heat today."

he said.

"What?" I asked.

"We're having a few problems firing it up."

It was now 4:00 P.M. and I knew that they only work until five. They had been here since 8:00 A.M. and I suspected that they were just about finished for the day. They still had to pack everything up and drive back to the shop before quitting time. "We'll be back tomorrow," the man said.

"The same time?" I asked.

"Yeah, but we need to send another guy out to take a look at it."

"Okay," I said. After all, what choice did I have?

That night I went to bed with no heat and extra blankets. It was okay. I made it through. But, the one dream that I had that night I have never gotten out of my mind. In fact it was the only dream I remember having out of the entire night.

The dream was very short but very clear. It was a dream about a red and green wire. It was a vivid image, like a picture of a red and green wire in front of a black background. Almost as if it was a large picture that had been framed and hung on a wall and I was standing there staring at it. It was right in front of my face. There was one basic root of a wire and then the wire would split at the ends with the red going to the left and the green going towards the right. When I was awakened the next morning, it was this image that I had in my head, and it wouldn't go away. It just seemed very odd to remember something as strange as this.

I woke up startled the next morning to a knocking on the front door. I looked out the bedroom window to see a heater truck parked along the street. I walked down the steps and opened the door. "Good morning," he said. "I'm here to

22

look at your heater."

"Are you the only one?" I asked. "I was expecting the same guys from yesterday."

"They were sent to another job," he explained.

"All right...well come in."

He followed me through the living room and into the dining room until I pointed toward the basement door. "The basement is right down there." I said.

He had a tool box in his hand and he walked down the basement stairs. After around fifteen minutes he came back up the steps with his tool box. "It's working," he said.

"It's working? Already?" I asked.

"Yeah, it's fired up. Just turn your thermostat up and you'll start to feel the warm air through the blower."

"What was wrong with it?" I asked.

"Ah, those guys yesterday hooked up the red and green wire wrong."

9.

Dim Lighting

A more personal experience happened during a night when I was feeling very depressed. I don't know why I kept sobbing that night, but the tears started to roll down my face around midnight and they wouldn't stop. I was sitting in the living room, had the tissue box on my lap, and was littering the floor with them. Feeling sad and hopeless I decided to go to bed.

I walked into the kitchen and turned out the overhead light, turned off the light to the bathroom and then walked over to the brown standing touch lamps that lay on the sideboard table alone the dining room wall. I had to touch each of these lamps three times in order for them to go off.

The way these lamps work is if I touch my hand on any piece of the metal, the lamp will go on. One touch will make the lamp dim, two touches will make it a little brighter, and three touches will turn the lamp on to its full brightness. A forth touch to the lamp will turn it off again and the cycle will then start all over.

Rarely do I activate these lamps more than the first touch. I usually like to keep the dining room dim to present an atmosphere.

One problem that I have though, is when the dining room windows are open and the wind blows, the wind will be strong enough to turn the left lamp on to a first touch or the lowest dim. This had happened a few times before but it is only the left lamp that goes on, never the right one. I guess the wind isn't strong enough to reach the other side of the table to activate the other one I would tell myself. This seemed to make sense to me.

After I touched each of these lamps to turn them off completely, I started upstairs to bed. Once in my bedroom, I plopped down onto my bed, pulled a blanket over me and tried getting to sleep.

The tears however kept coming. My sobs were louder. It seemed as if all of my emotions were just pouring out of me. After another sleepless hour, I needed to go to the bathroom. And since the only bathroom in the house is downstairs on the first floor, going to the bathroom is work.

Out of bed, down the stairs I went. I walked through the dark living room, through the dark dining room and into the bathroom.

When I came out of the bathroom though, I noticed that the room was a lot brighter than it was when I went into the bathroom. I then noticed that the left lamp on the sideboard table was on at its full brightness. I looked at it, walked over to it and then gave the lamp one touch. It went off as expected.

As I started to walk out of the room I said to myself, the wind must have been very strong to come through and turn that lamp on like that. I then turned to look at the two windows only to discover that they were both closed shut.

10.

Catherine

I knew that a two year old girl had died in this house from polio. I learned it from a woman who stopped by one day. I couldn't help thinking now, was this somehow related to some of the things that are going on in here.

It was in the early spring of the year 2001. Nancy and I hadn't met yet and Joey was around seven years old. I was having a yard sale in my front yard. It was a chilly Saturday morning and I had a few tables set up of my useless junk.

It was just before noon on that day when an older woman stopped by. I didn't see her get out of a car and I didn't see her walking down the street. I just looked up and it seemed like she was there. Her hair was silver and her movement was slow. I guessed her age to be in the mid seventies. I couldn't help wondering to myself why she would be interested in any of my things.

It wasn't long, after she scanned my tables, that she began to talk. It was then that I learned that it wasn't the sale that she was interested in, it was the house. When she was a young girl in the 1930's, she had lived in this house.

She introduced herself as Catherine and preceded to tell me stories about her living here. She told me that she and six other people lived in the house at the same time and that the rent in those days was $25.00 a month. She reminisced of the good times they had playing cards through the fence and playing mumblety-peg underneath the big old oak tree in the front yard.

At this time, no one else was at my sale, so I asked her if she would like to come in for a look. She was thrilled at the invitation and graciously accepted. We walked into the front door which led directly into the small enclosed porch. Upon entering I instantly could see a smile run across her face. "This is exactly how I remember it," she said.

As she stepped from the porch into the living room, her eyes immediately focused on the far wall where my couch now sits. As she pointed her finger she said, "This is the spot where the caskets were laid out."

"Caskets?" I asked.

"Yes, for the funerals," she responded.

My eyes suddenly became fixated on the spot of the room where she was pointing, and finally after a brief moment of silence the word finally came out of my mouth. "Funerals?" I asked.

"Well yes," she explained. "In those days they didn't have funeral parlors so funerals had to be held in peoples' houses."

My eyes were glued to this spot thinking to myself that this is the spot where I sit, read and watch T.V.

"Oh," I reacted, acting as if I wasn't bothered by it. "How many funerals were held here?" I asked carefully.

"Three that I can remember."

"Did you know them? Do you know who they were?" I asked.

"Oh yes, I knew them," she explained.

"Who were they?" I asked

"Well...it was a man, a woman, and a little two year old girl. The man had drowned. The woman died from an infection and the two year old girl died from polio."

27

"Really?" I asked.

"Yes," said Catherine. "In fact, the two year old girl died upstairs in your front bedroom."

"She did?" I asked.

"Oh yes, and you know what?" she said while chuckling. "The day that she died up in the bedroom was the same day that the garage burned to the ground." I simply stared at her listening to her every word. "It was then that my father thought that the house was jinxed and so shortly after we moved out."

We walked around the rest of the house and she told me a story about the room which was now the bathroom and how it used to be a pantry. She explained that there were beds everywhere. She then while looking out the backdoor, pointed to the spot where an outhouse had been. Catherine had a smile on her face the entire tour.

"Catherine," I asked. "What else can you tell me about the people who had their funerals here in my living room, the ones who died."

"Well, the man who had drowned, his name was George Dever. He was forty-one and such a nice man. He was a bridge worker-a night watchman. He worked for Easton Engineering. They are the ones who built the Ninth Street Bridge and the causeway entering into Ocean City. Well, one night he fell off of the cofferdam and went into the water. His body had been missing for four days. When they finally found him, they learned that he had fallen around 4:00 A.M. That's when his pocket watch had stopped."

"Really?" I said subtly.

"The woman, she was young. She was in her late twenties or early thirties. She developed an infection after a miscarriage and...they didn't have antibiotics in those days so...it was sad."

"That's terrible." I said.

"And Ginny, the two year old...well Virginia Murphy was her name. She was my sister. She died in December 1932 from polio. She was a delightful pretty little girl, no trouble at all. I remember she would untie shoelaces. You know I only have one little picture of her sitting on a bike. That's all I have of her."

"How old were you when she died?" I asked.

"Well I was born in 1924 and she died in 1932 so I was eight years old. Yes, that's right because Eddie was then born in your house in 1933."

"In what room was Eddie born?" I asked.

"He was born in the same room that Ginny died. And those bodies, they would be laid out there all night long. It was during the depression. It was a sad time and that's what they did in those days."

I don't know why I didn't take her upstairs. Maybe by this time I had heard enough. She went up on her own and looked around, but she was back down after a minute or so. She thanked me a few times, walked out the door and then went on her way. I then went and stood behind the tables of my yard sale with a very unsettling feeling.

The realization was starting to sink in that this could all be related. Is it all connected? There were dead bodies in my living room, a little girl died in the bedroom and in the meantime I have a bunch of strange things going on in here. Maybe one of these dead bodies has some attachment to this house that I didn't know about. Maybe one of them is very alive in spirit hanging around here. I didn't have any answers. All I had were more questions.

I've got strange things going on in here and I've got no explanation for any of it.

11.

They're Here

It wasn't long before I started to notice other strange things going on, particularly now in the bedroom where the two year old girl had died.

In the middle of the afternoon one day in early June, I went upstairs, laid down on the bed and the T.V. went on. At first I thought that I had sat on the remote control, until I glanced over and saw the remote control sitting on the night table.

In that same month, I arrived home from work around midnight and went up to the bedroom. I turned on the light only to find the toy boot of one of my son's action figures lying on the bed in the area where I sleep. My son hadn't been over in three days. What's peculiar about this is that ten hours before, I had sat in that very spot of the bed while getting ready for work. There was no toy boot on that bed. Just to confirm my suspicion, the next morning I called my son to ask him if he knew anything about it. He told me that all of his army guys were downstairs and that he hadn't played with them in a while.

In this same bedroom a Roland electronic piano sits on a stand. It goes on automatically. There are times when I go upstairs and the red power light is on. In one such incident, I sat down to play it after seeing the power light on, and just as I sat down to play, the light went off. Thinking that I had hit something while sitting down, I checked all of the connections and then checked them again. I could not get the power back. I turned the power switch off and walked away in frustration. One hour later I went back upstairs to get something only to notice the red power light was on again.

The most chilling time for me was when I had lost the remote control to the bedroom VCR. This remote control never leaves the room. I searched for it for days. I looked under the bed, all around the floor, looked through my clothes, and all around the night tables. I couldn't find it. I tore the room apart. It had been missing for two weeks and I had no idea where it could be. I eventually gave up.

There was one evening though when my son was over. He told me that he wanted to go upstairs and watch T.V. in my bedroom.

After about twenty minutes I went upstairs to check on him just to make sure everything was okay. I walked into the room to find him happy as can be. He was laying on his stomach with his head at the foot of the bed and feet towards the pillow watching the show Full House. It was obvious to me that he was fine and that there was no reason for me to worry about him or to be concerned.

"Hi Daddy," he said as I walked through the bedroom door.

"Hi Joe." I just thought I'd come up and check on you."

"Do you want to watch Full House with me?" he asked.

"No, I've got the dishes to do. I'm going to go down and work on them."

"Okay," said Joey.

"I'll see you in a little bit," I said as I started out the door.

"Bye Daddy."

Just as I turned to walk out of the bedroom door to go

31

back downstairs, I noticed something. I noticed that Joey had the lost VCR remote control in his hand. I immediately started questioning him as to where he got it. "Joey, where did you find that?" I asked insistently.

"What?" He asked, as if he had no idea what I was talking about.

"The remote control to the VCR. You're holding it. Where did you get that? Where did you find it? Where was it?"

He calmly turned onto his left side to look at me, and with a confused look on his face he spoke in a very matter of fact voice and said, "Dad, it was in the middle of the bed."

"What?" I asked.

"It was in the middle of the bed when I came up to watch T.V." he said.

Joey had no idea that the remote control had been lost and that I had been frantically searching for it for two weeks. The interesting thing is, that within the two weeks time of it being missing, I had stripped all of the bedding twice to wash the sheets.

12.

Work with the Clues

I was led to believe now that whoever is living here with us is somewhat of a practical joker. "There is definitely activity in this bedroom," I told Joey after that happened. We then both started to think about the things that have happened. They took and hid the VCR remote control from me only for it to be found again in the middle of the bed by you. They took my car keys from me only to be found again in the middle of the kitchen counter. They took the pretzels away, but gave you your snack first. They constantly play with the lights, the electric to the house, the piano, the CD player, and the T.V. And just tonight I spent a good three minutes trying to get that lamp working and it wouldn't go on. And now it's working.

"Really?" I just pulled the chain and it went on," said Joey.

But yet at the same time, whoever this is living with us, they also have compassion and are looking out for me. They were there for me the night I was sobbing. They knew that I was upset and they lit the light on the sideboard table as I was coming out of the bathroom.

And they were there for me during the cold nights when I had no heat. They tried to tell me what the problem was by communicating to me through a dream. They told me about the red and green wire even before the heater technician did. All I had to do was listen.

I can surmise to say that whoever this is, they are having fun with us. They are enjoying the teasing.

13.

Bedroom Wall

One morning during the summer of 2005, Joey and I woke up to physical evidence which could hold proof that this was in fact all real.

One night during the early part of that summer, Joey and I went to bed around 9:00 P.M. We both slept peacefully and somewhere during the night he had crawled into bed with me.

The next morning we awoke. I was still very groggy in my sleep when I heard him say, "Dad, look at this!"

"What? What is it?" I mumbled while still half asleep.

"On the wall!" Joey cried. "Look!"

I knew it was something serious. The sound of his voice was full of excitement. As I turned over to look at him I noticed that he was on his hands and knees on the bed facing the wall.

"What is it?" I asked.

"I don't know." he said.

When I finally got up to look at what he was looking at, I gasped. This woke me up much faster than a cup of coffee, and I now was also on my hands and knees examining it.

"Was this here last night?" I asked.

"No!" He confirmed.

"Are you sure?"

"Positive, I would have seen it." Joey said reassuringly.

On the wall was a pencil line six and a half feet long that had been drawn overnight. It stretched clear across the king size bed and ended at both ends of the night tables. It measured to be about two feet above our pillows.

"Wow!" I said to Joey.

"Do you think it was the ghost?" Joey asked.

"I don't know. I don't know how else it would have gotten there." I replied.

Around one week later, my sister Jane and her children Abigail and Alec visited. I took them upstairs to see the drawing on the wall and to get their impression of it. Jane was in total disbelief, and the children were very excited knowing that there was a ghost in the house.

Since then, I've invited other people to the bedroom to look at the wall. Everyone pretty much agreed that by the way that it was drawn, and with the king size bed in the way, that no human being could have done it. Even after many serious conversations discussing it, no one was able to provide a logical explanation as to how it got there.

14.

The Psychic, Monique

I remember that it was around this time that I wanted to get to the bottom of all this. I wanted some answers. It was hard for me to talk to people about it though because this can be very sensitive subject matter for some people. It is dangerous territory. Not everyone believes in ghosts, spirits, or an afterlife. The only way that someone would truly be able to identify with my situation would have to be someone who has gone through it themselves. Perhaps someone who is interested in the subject, is open to it, and won't act as a skeptic. I needed to talk to someone who could really understand and relate to it.

It was during an episode of the Montel Williams show that shed some new light and direction. The guest on the show that day was world renowned psychic Sylvia Browne. People from the audience were asking her questions about their loved ones who have died and were asking her if she could see them, could she connect with them, are they all right? On the spot, she was able to connect with the spirit world with her psychic abilities and give them the answers to the questions they were asking. She told one lady in the audience that the house that she was living in was built over an old Indian village and this was the reason why the woman was hearing voices, laughter, and would come home to find that objects had moved. The spirits were still at the village. It just happens to be her house now.

It was then that it occurred to me that maybe I should go to see a psychic. I was obsessed with what was going on in my house, and if I could talk to someone about it, and if they could give me some answers as to what was going on, then at least maybe I would be able to regain some of my sanity back.

I had never gone to a psychic before and I didn't know where to find one. I didn't know how much it costs, or how to tell if someone is really a psychic. I didn't want some fraudulent person trying to make a dishonest buck by telling me a bunch of nonsense. I was going through a real situation and I needed some real answers. I needed to find someone who had the "gift."

I quietly started asking friends if they knew anyone, and I kind of put the word out that I was looking, if anyone knew of anyone, but again this goes way beyond the comfort zone for a lot of people. I was also starting to see a pattern, that when you say the word psychic to people, they often will give some sort of facial expression, indicating disapproval.

I didn't know where to go for this. The people I asked offered no direction and my resources were running thin.

It was in the following week though, when I got a break. I overheard Beverly say that she and a few girls were going to take a trip to go see Monique. It suddenly clicked that Monique was a tarot card reader that Beverly had gone to in the past. Beverly is my first wife. We have been divorced for ten years. And during our marriage, I remember her saying at times that she was going to see Monique.

Apparently Beverly had already heard a lot about what was happening in the house from Joey. Beverly is Joey's biological mother. He had told her many of the stories, but I had never really talked to Beverly about it. We usually only talk about our son and trying to keep things "tight" in raising him. Conversations with Beverly were usually short and to the point, and the topic is always Joey. We really don't ask each other too many personal questions. This time however, I needed her. I needed her input and direction to this Monique person and what she might be able to do for me. I picked up the phone and called her.

Beverly was very receptive in my plea for help and became very interested in having me go to see her. "I think she can really help you," she said. Beverly offered to drive because she knew the way as well as the routine of how things worked once we got there.

No date had been set yet, but at least I was one step closer to maybe finding out what was going on in my house. All I had to do now was to prepare myself for what I was going to say and what I was about to hear.

15.

The Coffee House on the Corner

I was very apprehensive about going. Or, maybe I should say that I was very afraid about going. I had never been read by a psychic before and I was very nervous about it. Something about it just didn't seem natural to me. I think that I was very afraid of what this person was going to say. Would she think that I was crazy for thinking that I am experiencing the things that I am? Would she attack my character and who I am as a human being? Is it possible that I could come out of the meeting feeling even more afraid than before I went in? Or, could she actually give me a logical explanation for these strange things happening in my home. There were so many unanswered questions and I had a growing sense of anxiety. I decided that whatever was going to happen, I didn't want to wait any longer. I wanted to know as soon as possible.

Within a week Beverly and I agreed that she would drive. She would pick me up at my house that following Thursday around 4:00 P.M. and we would get there around quarter to five. It was a good forty, forty-five minute drive.

A few days later she came. She was right on time. I got in the car, and we started up the road.

During the car ride I was feeling very nervous and uncomfortable. I started thinking things like, is this going to change my perspective on life? Would she tell me things like, stay away from all blue cars for the next six months, or that I am going to develop a sudden illness and only have three years to live! Was I really ready to hear things like that?

No, I told myself. I don't want to hear any of those things. It was then that I decided that I only wanted to know about the house. I only want to know what is going on in the house. I don't want her to tell me anything about my personal life. I'm just not interested.

"This is it!" announced Beverly. We had arrived. I raised my head to see a coffee house on the corner of a town's business district in central New Jersey. "She works out of here." Beverly confirmed.

She then explained to me that Monique will come in and sit at a small table in the back. Anyone who wants to be read needs to write their name on the chalkboard by the entrance way and then she will call you in the order that the names appear. "We're going to try and be first," she said.

We were there early so we decided to sit down at a table and order something. We each got a sandwich. Beverly then gave me a little background information. "Monique is only here three days a week from 6:00 to 9:00 P.M. The chalkboard get filled up very quickly with people wanting to be read. The problem is, even though the readings last only fifteen or twenty minutes long, if you get behind five or six other people on the list then you have to wait around. That's why it's good to get here early."

"Which person is she?" I asked.

"She's not here yet," she said. "I'll tell you when she comes in."

While sitting at the table waiting for our sandwiches to be delivered, I couldn't help noticing the other people who strolled in and wrote their name on the chalkboard. There was no one of any certain age or gender. It was both women and men, young and old. Some would write their name and then sit at the counter to have coffee or a latté, some sat at a table to eat, and some simply wanted to put their name on the board, only to leave again and come back when they felt it was closer to their turn. One thing was for sure, a lot of people know that Monique is here and they come to see her.

"At least we're first." Beverly said as she looked around the restaurant.

"I only want to know about the house you know." I said.

"I know," she said. "And I'm sure she will tell you everything that she can about it."

"I really hope that I haven't been imagining all of this, the stuff going on in my house."

"We'll, we're going to find out," she said.

"If she tells me that there is absolutely nothing going on in my house then I am going to need you to take me right to a therapist."

Beverly laughed. "Oh," she said. "After she gives you your reading you are allowed to ask her three questions.

"Okay," I said.

As I took my last bite of chicken salad and scraped my plate of the last potato chip, Beverly slowly leaned towards me and in a soft voice said, "There she is. She's the woman in black."

She was a small to medium sized woman. She was of Indian decent and had piercings through her ears and her nose. Her outfit was a long dress of a dark color. Her back was towards me so it was difficult to notice anything without staring. She walked to the end of the counter and ordered a cup of coffee. "This is what she always does," said Beverly. "It's kind of her routine. She'll come in, get a coffee, sit a minute, and will then go to the back to get herself set up. Then she'll call the first name."

"Does she know that we are first?" I asked nervously.

"Yes," Beverly comforted me. "I saw the waitress tell her and then the waitress motioned over to me."

Within a minute or so the waitress delivered our check and assured us that Monique knows that we are at the top of the list. "Thank you." Beverly and I said at the same time.

I knew now that the time was growing near. The negative pessimistic thoughts were a constant reminder. Is she for real? Will she tell me if she sees death? Can she predict the future?

I convinced myself not to give her any information. I'm not going to volunteer anything I said to myself. I will just sit back and let her tell me things. Let me see what she says and what she knows, then I'll decide for myself if she's for real or not.

With that, I noticed that she had gotten off of her stool at the counter. She had picked up her large bag that she had brought in with her and started walking towards the back of the coffee shop. I watched her pull out a navy blue table cloth and drape it over the small table for two in the back corner. She then pulled a few other things out of her bag while she continued to get herself organized. Minutes later, I looked up to find her standing at our table.

"Hi," said Beverly.

"Hi," said Monique in a soft, soothing voice. "You're first right?" she asked.

"Yes," Beverly responded. "Well...Greg is, I'm not going to get read today."

"Oh, okay," said Monique. "Why don't we get you started then. Come on back."

I got up from the table and followed her back to the corner. I sat down, folded my hands on the blue table cloth and waited. She fixed her long dress and then sat down across from me.

"This is my first time," I nervously announced.

"First time with me?" she asked.

"No, first time ever to be read by anyone." I told her.

"...And it's a full moon," she said sarcastically.

Right away she relaxed me. I guess I never thought that psychics had a sense of humor. I guess I thought that they were too busy talking to the dead or doing whatever it is that they do. Anyway, she relaxed me with her soft tone and her joke. It helped put me at ease to the point where I gave a little smile.

Monique held the tarot cards in her hand. Once I saw them, I quickly unfolded my hands and removed them from the table. Monique spread the tarot cards across the table in a fan formation and told me to put my hands on them to spread my energy. She then directed me to concentrate on thirteen cards and to pick them out. One by one she then started to flip over the cards that I had picked. I had no idea what was going through her mind but it was obvious that she was concentrating. One by one she was flipping the cards over and laying them spread out on the table, but by the fifth card she still hadn't said a word. I was getting increasingly nervous. She then turned over the sixth card, and then the seventh, still with no words to say. She was very quiet. It wasn't until after the eighth card when she began to speak. "This is interesting," she said. "There is nothing here that would indicate that you have any trouble with your job, career, or money. It seems that this area of your life at this time is intact and that they are not a concern of yours in anyway."

I sat very still and quiet. I didn't react to any of the things that she had just told me. She never looked up at me. She looked down and focused her eyes on the cards. I just let her keep on talking. "It does say however, that you have many personal problems. In fact I'm seeing personal problems all over these cards." She continued to turn the remaining cards over. I sat without saying a word. Having her expose my personal life was not the reason that I was there. One thing was for sure though, I do have to admit, she's pretty accurate so far.

With me not confirming in anyway that she was right, she continued on. "It seems that you have just come off of something big, something major. There was a battle of some sort," she said. "You have just come out of a big battle."

"Wow!" I thought to myself. She's talking about my recent divorce to my second wife. Yes, it was horrible. How does she know that? It *was* a battle. It was a bitterly contested divorce.

Okay, I was impressed. She had spoken so few words but they were remarkably accurate. I had just come off of my second divorce which was an eight month legal battle between two lawyers. It was one of the most awful things that I had ever been through. It was very expensive and a very stressful time of my life. How interesting it was for her to pick up on that right away. She's for real, I told myself.

She continued to talk and I kept listening. "I can't even go into detail about your personal life," she said. "It is so broad and so vast, it is all over the place." I continued to listen. "What you should be doing now is laying low," she advised. "Whatever you try and push for at this time of your life is going to fail. Things will open up for you, but not yet. Lay low and let everything around you fall into place. Things *will* and *are* going to get better for you. Sit back and let them happen. They will happen."

This was all that she could tell me. It was very general, but also very accurate. My personal life had been a mess over the last year or so and she was able to see it with her ability. That's amazing, I thought to myself.

"I understand that I can ask you questions?" I asked.

"Yes, What would you like to know?" she asked.

"Well, I'm having trouble with my house. I'm having things appearing and disappearing. Is there anything you can tell me about that?"

She gathered up all of her tarot cards, straightened them and then once again spread them out on the table in a fan formation. She then directed me to choose seven cards. She turned them over and quietly looked at them. The awkward moments of silence felt like hours. She was very deep in thought, and I couldn't imagine what she was going to come out with. She then began to tell.

"Well...you definitely have an older woman living with you."

"I do?" I reacted.

"Yes, oh...and...I see children. There are children. There are two children that visit you."

"What?" I asked.

"This woman living with you however is not these children's mother. She watches them...like a nanny. This woman also never owned the house. She just lives there while taking care of these children."

She then paused until a smile came upon her face. "They love you!" She said as her smile grew larger. "And they love you living in the house. They also love what you have done with the house."

What? I thought to myself. My heart was pounding heavier. I've been working on that house since the day I moved in. You mean they know that? They can see that? I simply sat there astonished. All of this time it hasn't been my imagination. I do have a ghost in this house, and not one...but three.

Monique paused and then went on. "One of the children loves to draw," she confirmed. "You may want to start focusing on mirrors, windows, walls or dirt outside the house. The other child leaves you gifts. Have you ever come across anything in your house and asked yourself, where did this come from?"

Monique then paused before telling me more. "This older woman living with you is worried," she explained. "She is afraid that you are going to want her to leave. She is afraid that you are not going to want her there, that you are going to send her away."

"I'm not going to do that," I responded softly.

"Also, this woman...she likes to entertain. She has parties...but mostly for the children."

"Okay," I said softly.

"She had a very peaceful death. She died of natural causes. There was no pain at all in her passing."

"Is she earthbound?" I asked. "Does she know that she is dead? Does she have unfinished business here on earth?"

"No, she is not earthbound. She's crossed over." Monique answered. "She really wants to talk to you. She really wants to tell you some things." Monique said.

"She wants to talk to me?" I asked. "Talk to me about what? What does she want to talk to me about?" I asked.

"She wants you to slow down."

"She wants me to slow down?" I asked.

"I'm trying to get a name for you," she continued. "It sounds like it starts with an 'E'. I'm getting a very strong 'E' she said.

"Is the name Evelyn?" I asked excitedly.

"I don't know. I can't get it," she explained.

While driving home in the car from the coffee shop and the reading, I immediately began to write everything down on a piece of paper. I wanted to write down what she had told me just as I remembered it. At my request, Beverly sat quietly and drove the car. Once I finished writing, Beverly asked the question that I could now confirm to be true.

"So, do you have a ghost?" she asked.

"Yes," I responded. "I have a ghost."

16.

Making Sense of It All

"Who is this Evelyn?" Beverly asked.

"Evelyn is the eighty-two year old widow that I bought the house from. She must have died. She and her husband owned the house for thirty-nine years. The last twelve years though she lived there alone. This was the woman who referred to me as the gentleman who likes older houses," I explained. "I remember Lou Ann from next door telling me the story of when they found her lying on the living room floor unable to get up."

"Really? And they found her?"

"Yes," I said. "Lou Ann just happened to go over there. She knocked on the door and when no one answered she peaked through the window and saw her. Apparently she had been lying there for two hours unable to get herself off of the floor."

"That's terrible," said Beverly.

"I know. Then after selling the house to me, she moved into the assisted living housing in Ocean City. That's the last time I heard about her. And coincidentally enough, it was two years ago that they tore down the assisted living building, which was right around the time when strange things started happening in my house."

"So you think it's her?" Beverly asked.

"I don't know. It's starting to make sense. She must have been heartbroken. It was such a shame for her because she sold the house that she loved, the house that held thirty-nine years of her memories only to move into a retirement home thinking that it was the right thing for her to do, and then they tore down the retirement home. She had to move again. This is not how you want to spend the last years of your life."

"It does make sense that she would want to come back to live in her old house again, which is your house now," said Beverly.

"Monique said that she couldn't get a definite name but she got a very strong 'E' as the first letter." I said factually.

"That is a coincidence," said Beverly.

"But the pieces of the puzzle fit." I said convincingly. "I think Evelyn has passed away and came back home to live in her house–the one I'm in now. She loved this house. She spent many happy years here, and this house has the last memories of her husband. The older woman that Monique was referring to is Evelyn. She came back home."

Two days had passed when I ran into Lou Ann, my neighbor. I was pulling into my driveway when I saw her. I stopped the car just after pulling in as she was out in the front yard loading some things into her car. I rolled down the passenger side window and called out, "Hi, Lou Ann!"

"Hi Greg," she said with a wave.

"Lou Ann, could I talk with you a minute? Could I ask you something?"

Lou Ann walked over to my car and I began to tell her the story that I had some strange things happening in my house. I told her that I had gone to a psychic to see if I could find anything out.

"What's happening?" she asked. "What's going on? What kind of strange things?"

"Well...it's mostly things appearing and disappearing," I told her.

"I'll have to get my sister to come over," said Lou Ann. "She'll go through the house for you."

"Oh, is your sister into that kind of stuff?" I asked.

"Yes, it's what she does for a living. She's a channeler. It's going to be a little while though. We just found out that her son was killed in a motorcycle accident a couple of days ago. The funeral is in two days. She's not doing too well right now."

"Oh, man...that's terrible."

"Yeah, things are a bit of a mess here right now. If she's doing okay, the next time she comes down from New York, I'll mention it to her."

"Thanks," I said. "But Lou Ann, the psychic that just read me said that there is an older woman living with me. I think that it might be Evelyn. Evelyn loved this house and they recently tore down the assisted living home where she was living. I think she came back as a spirit to live in her home again. I think that the woman I have living here with me is Evelyn. What do you think?"

"No," she said. "No, it's definitely not Evelyn."

"No? You don't think so? How can you be sure it's not Evelyn? It all makes perfect sense." I said.

"Because," she said with a laugh. "Evelyn is still alive."

17.

Deeds for Leads

My theory got rained on. Evelyn is still alive. This means that I now have no idea who this woman is living with me, why she is here, and what she could possibly want to talk to me about. She wants me to slow down. Slow down with what? Slow down with work? Slow down my life? Should I be exercising more? What does that mean?

I decided to take my chances at the county deeds office. I figured that if I knew who had lived in the house before me, maybe it would give me a lead.

I went to the deeds office at the local county court house office building and started tracing back all of the signed deeds by the owners of this house. It was there that I learned that the house was built in 1904 and before the year 1920 the house had already changed hands eight times.

In 1920 the house was sold to a Mr. and Mrs. Frank Peiffer. They owned the house for close to nineteen years until they sold it in 1938.

The buyer then, was a single woman by the name of Louise Coulson. She owned the house for six years. She then sold it in 1944.

Harold and Martha Hargreaves were the ones that bought it. Martha however, died in 1948 and Harold sold the property in 1950. He sold it to Edward and Elaine Thorton. The Thorton's kept it for eleven years until they sold it in 1961.

In May of 1961, Ralph and Evelyn Booger bought it.

Ralph and Evelyn Booger owned the house the longest out of anyone. They owned it for thirty-nine years. Ralph died in 1988 and twelve years after that Evelyn moved into an assisted living housing program. She sold the house to Gregory Young. Gregory Young bought the house in the year 2000 and still resides in it today.

Having this information was interesting but it wasn't long before I realized that it wasn't going to help me in my pursuit for answers. Monique had distinctly said that the woman never owned the house.

So now instead of having answers, I only had more questions. Did this woman rent the house? Was she paid to watch it for someone? And what about the children? Was she the caretaker of these children? Was she paid to watch these children? And if so, which of the owners did she work for?

An acquaintance once mentioned to me that in the 1920's and 1930's wealthy families from Pennsylvania would sometimes send a nanny and the children down to the shore for the summer. This, I was lead to believe was common place at that time. The nanny would be the caretaker for those children during the summer months. Then, when September arrived, the nanny and children would go back to Pennsylvania to rejoin with the parents.

The problem is, even if this is indeed the scenario, there is no record of it. There is no way to prove it, and these children would be well in their eighties if they were still alive. The nanny would have died years ago. So hypothetically if these children are still alive, then these certainly aren't the children who are ghosting around my house.

I was confused. None of this added up. I had a hunger for this knowledge but was only getting crumbs at a time. Trying to piece together who lived here and which ghosts lived with which people I thought to be an impossible task. I finally accepted the fact that I had hit a dead end, and accepted the fact that I will never know the story behind all of this.

Nevertheless, I continued to document all of the strange occurrences that kept happening and I hoped that one day answers would eventually come. In reality though, my hopes were dim.

If only I could clear my mind of it all. If I could just get it out of my head. But, I can't. I'm always thinking about it. It consumes all of my thoughts. These ghosts, they know I'm here, they see me, they hear me, and they love what I have done with the house. I, on the other hand, know nothing about them. I can't see them, I can't hear them, I only know that objects have moved, the electricity is constantly played with, and the lights...they are always playing with the lights. This is as far as I've gotten.

At this point, my guess would be that it is the children that are the ones teasing me and playing with things and the woman is the one who looks after me. Could it be that she didn't like my second wife? Did she want her to leave? Did she push her down the basement stairs? Did she purposely knock the Christmas tree over to break the angel heads that my wife loved so much? Was she trying to put forth a message? After all, Nancy did say, "There is something in this house and it doesn't like me." How can you sense something like that? I had no answers. I kept digging and digging only to find nothing but more questions.

That was, however, until I struck gold. I met Lou Ann's sister, the channeler from New York.

18.

She Can See Them

I knew that I had never seen her before. I've lived here for five years but have never seen this woman. I've had many conversations with Lou Ann over these years, but I never knew that she had a sister. It turns out that she has four sisters. Maybe I just don't ask the right questions.

The first time I saw her she was standing on the back deck of Lou Ann's house. I was watching from my kitchen window which overlooks the backyards of my property and Lou Ann's property.

I didn't know any of the details of her son's motorcycle accident. I only knew that he had been recently killed and that it was bad, really bad, and was a shock to everyone.

I personally am horrible in trying to console people in those situations. I never know what to say. What do you say? What could you possibly say to comfort them or to make them feel better? And, is that what you are supposed to do, make them feel better?

I tied up the trash bag and went out the backdoor towards the alley. I dumped the trash in the can and then started back toward the house. While passing the birdbath, I noticed it was dry and decided to fill it. Lou Ann's sister had her back to me the entire time. She was about seventy-five feet away standing in one spot on Lou Ann's deck. I looked up at her once or twice, but just went about my business.

I filled the birdbath and started to go back inside

when I heard a call from across the yard.

"How's your ghost?" she called out.

"Oh...okay I guess." I called back to her.

She then started to walk closer to where I was standing. "Lou Ann said that you thought you had something going on," she said with a smile on her face.

"Yeah, I'm pretty sure I do," I said shyly.

She continued to walk closer toward me until the deck's railing stopped her. I then walked towards her until the chain linked fence separating the properties stopped me. "Yeah, I've got some things going on. It's a case of things appearing and disappearing." I explained. "I was told by a psychic that I've got a woman living with me but I don't know. I mean it's okay. There isn't really anything mean going on. It's a lot of small stuff. I guess the day that I have pots and pans flying around my kitchen is the day that I'll put up a 'for sale' sign. Are you Lou Ann's sister?" I asked.

"Yes, I'm here visiting. I'm thinking about moving back to the area but right now I'm just hanging out here for a while."

The woman was trying to be friendly but she did not look happy. I suppose who could after losing a child? I didn't say much, but I tried to make whatever I said meaningful and sincere. "I'm sorry to hear about your son."

She nodded. "I kept telling him to slow down or you're going to get hurt," she said. "He loved that bike. He lost control of it and ended up crashing into the guardrail. I kept telling him to be careful. If you don't have a body, you can't get well, no matter how hurt you are."

She then told me about the accident. Even though she wasn't there, she was able to tell me exactly how the accident happened. She was able to see it and describe it in detail.

While on the verge of tears, but chuckling at the same time, she said, "And after the mangled bike had finally come to a stop after throwing him a hundred feet away, my son rose up from his body, looked around, brushed himself off and said, 'What was that?' He didn't know that he had been killed."

"He loved that bike," she said. "I've been able to contact him only briefly and all that he wants to know is what I did with the bike? Where is the bike? I know that this will eventually pass but right now this is all that he cares about, and is all that he is saying to me. He wants to know why I gave the bike away, and why I didn't keep it."

"I couldn't keep it," she explained. "It was destroyed. And, because it would be a constant reminder of my son's death, I didn't want to keep it. But for some reason, this is what he cares about right now. He wants to know why I let them take it away."

I introduced myself as Greg and she told me that her name was Sharon.

Sharon has the psychic "gift" of seeing and communicating with the dead. From an early age, she had the ability to speak with energies, ghosts, and spirits. Her helper is her spiritual guide named Ma-Ryah, (pronounced Mariah). Ma-Ryah will use Sharon's body to enter our world and communicate. She can then relay information from other dimensions and other worlds. This is called channeling. Channeling is purported communication by a disembodied entity through a living person. Sharon is the living person. Sharon is the medium, or the deliverer of the messages that she is able to receive from the other side. Sharon is therefore and respectfully known as the "vessel."

This is Sharon's career. She is a professional channeler. She was a fascinating woman and she talked about her psychic ability very openly. She seemed to be very down to earth, sensitive and honest.

I also felt very bad for her. I couldn't imagine what she was going through. It seemed like she wanted to talk about her son's accident which surprised me. I tried to put myself on a level as to understand what she was going through, but who can? No one can ever understand the loss of a child unless they have gone through it themselves. I did the best I could in trying to be consoling and to listen, and to do my best to understand.

After a little while, the conversation began to drift. She told me about her place in New York, and a bit more about herself, and how she used to live in New Mexico. The conversation started to jump from one subject to another. We would talk about her, then back to her son and the accident, then to her life in New York, why she left New Mexico and so on.

All the while though, I was dying to ask her about my house and if she sensed anything about it. I thought that it might be inappropriate considering the circumstances of her recent trauma, but I was dying to ask her.

About forty minutes into our conversation, I decided to ask. After all, she had been facing the house the whole time that we had been talking. I decided to go for it.

"So I went to see a psychic a little while ago and she told me that I have an older woman living with me." I said.

"Yes, yes you do have an older woman living with you. Her name is Agnes."

"Her name is Agnes?" I asked.

"Yes, she goes by Agnes."

I started to watch Sharon's eyes. She was glancing at the house but looking away at the same time. I knew that Sharon was going to tell me more.

There became a few moments of silence. It wasn't an uncomfortable silence, just a bit of quiet. Sharon then started to look right into my eyes. It was almost as if she was looking through me. Her eyes seemed to be piercing through mine. Her voice then began to get soft and she was speaking much quieter now than moments before.

"This woman living with you, she's small...she's petite," said Sharon.

"She is?" I asked.

Sharon's eyes then glanced toward the house. "...And she wears her hair up."

Sharon took both of her hands, raised them and showed me how the woman wears her hair.

"...And she has wrinkles on her face," she said.

"Really?" I asked. "How old do you think she is?"

"She is about seventy years old."

Sharon then glanced away to look at the house. I was totally amazed by what she was telling me but with a curious chuckle I asked, "How do you know all of this?"

"Because," she said. "She is standing at the kitchen window watching us."

I didn't turn around and I didn't speak a word. I just kept staring at Sharon and watched her eyes. After a long pause I asked, "So she lives with me?"

"Yes. I can only see her from here up (pointing to the bottom of her rib cage) because the sink and counter are blocking."

"Is she with me all of the time?" I asked.

"Yes, she likes it here."

"She does?" I asked. "Is there a way for me to tell if she is here? How would I know?"

"She said she will touch you if you would like."

"She will touch me?" I asked.

"Yes, she will touch you here." Sharon points to her left shoulder.

"She will touch me on my left shoulder?"

"Yes, at times she will," said Sharon.

"Do you see any children?" I asked. "Are there any children that are here?"

"Yes, and they are the ones causing the problem with things appearing and disappearing or whatever games they are playing. It is them doing it."

"Wow!" I reacted. My jaw dropped in disbelief. Sharon then returned to her regular speaking voice.

"My advice is to treat them like they are real children," said Sharon. Acknowledge the joke that they are playing with you and give them a, 'ha, ha, that was a good one.' But, if they really start to get to you tell them that it is inappropriate for them to do that, and they will listen. Just be firm and direct and they will stop."

"Do you see any other spirits living here?" I asked.

"No, but that doesn't mean that there won't be," she said. "Your house kind of has a welcome mat outside inviting other ghosts to visit and pass through. But, just to warn you, it's like inviting people in off of the street. Not all of them are nice. Not all of them are going to be friendly or of a positive nature. If you ever sense something dark or negative you can call on Ma-Ryah and she will come help you."

"You mean, I can call on your spiritual guide and she will come to help me?"

"Yes, she will help you. Just call out to her, tell her

what the problem is and she will lead them out of your house."

"Do I have a spiritual guide?" I asked.

"Yes, everyone does."

"Can you tell me anything about my spiritual guide?" I asked.

Sharon began to again focus with her eyes locked into mine with a piercing look. She became quieter than in the voice which she was just speaking, but not as quiet when she was speaking of Agnes. She then took her eyes off of mine and started to look over my shoulder.

"He is right behind you," said Sharon.

"He? You mean it is a he...a man?"

"Yes and he is very tall. You come up to his shoulders. In a past life he was your brother. You called him John. He has green eyes...and white hair. You two have walked many lives together. It is in this life however that you have been separated. You came to be on earth and John is the one watching over you."

"Is he with me all of the time?" I asked.

"Yes, guides are with you from birth to birth. Humans see it as birth to death, but it is really birth to birth. This is when you cross over."

"Is there a way that I can tell if he is with me?" I asked.

Sharon paused and focused intently. "He will put his hand on your face...the left side of your face. If you feel your face getting warm or feel pressure on it, it is him doing it. He has his hand on you right now. Do you feel it?"

"Also, the smell of fresh cut grass is also an indication that he is with you. That's funny," she said with a

60

laugh. "There is always a smell associated with a spiritual guide and for you, for some reason, yours is the smell of fresh cut grass."

"He's gone now," said Sharon.

"You're a fascinating woman," I said.

"Thanks, but not everybody thinks so. It ruined my marriage and many times people look at me strange because they see me as talking to myself when actually I'm talking to Ma-Ryah, or I've connected with someone else."

"Wow! What do you do in those situations?"

"These days I just pull out my cell phone and act like I'm talking on it."

Sharon and I then talked about the improvements that I had made to the house and why I had cut down the tree that was on the side. I told her that if fell down during a bad storm. We talked about her son a little bit more and then we parted ways.

"It was great to meet you and talk to you," I said.

She then turned to go inside with her dog named Angel and I started up my back deck to enter through my backdoor.

"If you ever want me to come through your house, I'd be happy to do it," she offered as we were walking away from each other."

"Yes, I would love that," I called back to her.

19.

The Visit

It was a while before I saw Sharon again. She had gone back to New York and I had no idea when she would be coming back to visit her sister. I did however get a chance to talk to Lou Ann.

These days I hardly ever see Lou Ann. I live right next door to her but don't see her out in the yard nearly as much as I used to. She and her husband are so busy with their store and their other activities that I rarely see them out in the yard. I did however, run into her at the town flea market at the fire house parking lot. She was flipping burgers and turning hotdogs on the grill to raise money for the volunteer fire department. I made sure I said hello, and I really wanted to talk to her about her sister.

"Hi Lou Ann," I said.

"Hey stranger," she said.

"So I met Sharon, did she tell you?" I asked.

"Yeah, she did. She told me about your house. She's wild isn't she?"

"Oh man, the things she was telling me...I couldn't believe it." I said.

"She could blow you away with some of the things she could tell you," Lou Ann said. "She has blown me away many times."

"Has she always had this gift, this psychic ability?" I asked.

"Yes she has," said Lou Ann.

"She was incredible. Is she coming back to visit soon?" I asked.

"Yeah, I think she is going to leave New York and stay with us for a while. My other sister Linda is going to stay with us too. But I think Sharon wants to be around here permanently now. I think she wants to stay in this area."

"I'm going to ask her to come through my house when I see her again."

"Go ahead, she'll do it," said Lou Ann.

"All right, I'll let you get back to what you were doing. I'll see you later."

"All right, see ya," she said.

Over a month had gone by now since Sharon had been there. That was, until one day, when coming home from work, I noticed her car parked in front of Lou Ann's house. "She must be here," I said out loud to myself.

I knew at this time that I wanted to invite her over but I felt like I needed an excuse. I didn't just want to say, "Hey do you want to come over and tell me everything that is happening in my house without me paying you a dime." After all, people pay her to do what she does, and so far I haven't given her a cent. She read me in the backyard for free and now I am about to ask her to go through my house and tell me what she sees and what is going on in there for free. I guess I felt a little funny about it.

After giving it some thought, I decided that I would ask her over to look at the long pencil line that had mysteriously appeared on the bedroom wall. Maybe she would have some insight as to what it might be or where it came from. I was going to paint the room anyway, so actually it would be perfect if I could get her to look at this before I paint. "Okay," I told myself. "I have my plan." Now I need to find Sharon.

A few days had gone by. I kept a look out for her but didn't see her. I would see her dog Angel out in the yard, and saw her car parked out front, so I knew that she was there, but we both needed to be outside in the yard at the same time for it to be comfortable for me. I was not going to go knocking on their door to look for her or pester her.

It wasn't long, maybe the day after, when I had gotten home from work. I pulled the car into the driveway and saw Sharon outside on the deck talking on her cell phone. I waved hello and then walked in my backdoor. I did what I had to do in the house, but at the same time I kept an eye on her through the kitchen window waiting for her to hang up. It was then that I would ask her to come over. After a few short minutes, she hung up her phone, and she didn't go inside. She continued to stand on the deck and watch her dog run around in the yard. "Now is the time," I thought to myself. I walked out my backdoor to go talk to her.

"Sharon," I called out.

"Hi," she said.

"I was wondering if I could ask you something."

"Sure, what?" she asked.

"Well, I'm getting ready to paint my upstairs bedroom but there is something that I would like you to see first. There is something on my wall and I wanted to see what your take is on it. Do you mind coming over to take a look?"

"Sure, just give me a minute."

Sharon put Angel inside and started to walk around the front of the house. She walked around the chain linked fence which separates the properties and then started walking towards my backyard. I greeted her in the middle of the yard and we started walking towards my backdoor together.

"I appreciate you doing this," I said.

"Oh, it's no problem," she said. "I wanted to tell you anyway that Agnes was outside the other night."

"She was?" I asked.

"Yes, I was talking to her a little bit. I'm trying to get the names of the children for you."

"What was she doing outside?" I asked.

"I don't know what she was doing, but she was out there. I asked her what the names of the children were and she turned her head away from me, almost to look at them, and then she turned her head back, looked right at me and said, 'they don't want you to know'."

Sharon and I walked up the steps and onto the back deck. We then went into the backdoor which leads directly into the kitchen. We walked through the dining room, then the living room and up the stairs to the bedroom. Once we got in the bedroom I pointed to the pencil line and asked her what she thought.

"Wow!" she said with a giggle. She looked at the line and then held her hand over it at different sections. "Well, there is definitely more energy on the line than there is on the rest of the wall," she said.

She then held her hand over the line again—longer this time. Suddenly she broke into a big smile.

"One of the kids is drawing," she said. "He drew it."

"He did?"

"When you paint your room, just tell him not to draw on the walls anymore, and he won't," she said.

"So he drew it!" I said.

"Yep, it was him." Sharon then looked around the room. "Boy, this room has changed," she said.

"Yeah," I said. "I gutted the whole thing and started over."

"It looks good," she said. "It's been years since I've been in this house."

"Oh, so you have been in here before?" I asked.

"Oh yeah, I was in here a few times when Evelyn owned it. You have really done a lot with it," said Sharon.

"But Sharon," I said very seriously, "a two year old girl died in this room from polio. Is this the same child that is drawing on my wall?"

"No," she confirmed. "It's not."

I guess I felt relieved that it wasn't the two year old that had died up there but at the same time I still felt very confused. "Who is it then?" I asked myself. "Who are these kids? And, if Sharon was in this house before, did she ever sense anything before? Does she know more than she is telling me? What is she not telling me?"

We then walked back down the stairs and went into the kitchen. She looked around and marveled over the job that I had done and how nice it looked. "You're really neat for a guy," she said. "You keep your house very neat."

"Thanks," I said.

"So Sharon," I asked. "Is everyone still with me? It seems like nothing has happened for a few weeks now. No lights, no tricks, it's been quiet around here. Is everyone still here?" I asked.

"Oh yeah," she said. "In fact the boy was at the top of the staircase when I walked in."

"What? Where?" I reacted.

"Here, I'll show you," she said.

We walked out of the kitchen, back through the

dining room and stood at the base of the staircase. "He was standing right next to the table," she said.

"Really?"

"Yes, he has something wrong with his legs. There is a problem with his legs."

"There is?" I asked.

"I don't know where the girl is," said Sharon.

"The girl?" I asked excitedly. "So it's a boy and a girl?"

"Yes, and it's not the polio kid," she again confirmed.

At this time Sharon was walking to different sections of the living room and dining room and I was following her around like a puppy.

"You probably pass through his body a lot. Did you ever feel like you were hitting a soft sponge for a moment when walking up the steps? If so, you are passing through," she said.

"There have been a couple of times when I was walking up the steps, maybe it was two or three o'clock in the morning when I found myself starting to fall back a bit. I had to grab onto the railing to catch my fall," I explained.

"Just ask them to pass through. It's polite."

"How can I tell?" I asked.

"Bring your hands together like this with your fingers spread apart. Now move them away from each other and then bring them close together again. Do it over and over again. There is a point when they will tend to repel each other or feel spongy. This is the feeling that you will feel right before you pass through. It has to be practiced. It has to be developed, but over time you will feel it," explained Sharon.

"So Agnes is here with us right now too?" I asked.

"Yes, but Agnes spends most of her time in the kitchen. She will walk into the dining room, but not very far. She then will turn around and walk back into the kitchen. This is where she is most comfortable."

"Will I ever get to see Agnes?" I asked.

"If you do, it will be through your peripheral vision. She is not going to appear right in front of you. You have to look to your sides. Normally a spirit will start out behind you. Have you ever gotten the feeling that someone was watching you and you turn to look but no one is there? They start out behind you. Then in time, they will go more toward your sides. For me, and after doing it for so long, I can see them right in front of me. You'll see, one day Agnes just might surprise you," she said.

"Do you think that Agnes and the kids will be staying here a long time?" I asked.

"Yes I do. This is a very friendly and warm place. There is nothing bad going on here."

"And Agnes isn't earthbound?" I asked.

"No. She definitely has crossed over...she chooses to be here. She likes it here."

"Can she be other places too, at the same time?" I asked.

"Oh yes, she can be many different places at once and this is one of the places that she likes to be."

"Thank you Sharon."

"Well thanks for showing me your place," she said.

Sharon then walked out the backdoor, walked down the steps of the deck and started around the chain linked fence to go home.

I stood in the kitchen for a few minutes alone trying

to absorb and process what she had seen and what she had described to me.

It then suddenly occurred to me that there was something that I had forgotten to ask her about. There was something else that had been on my mind beside the pencil line that I wanted to get her input on. It was the vomit smell coming from in front of the dining room window. It was horrible. I had forgotten to ask her about it, and by this time she was already back inside her house.

A day or two later, Sharon left again to go back to New York. I then started on my next big construction project. I completely gutted my son's bedroom down to studs and decided to start over, beginning with new electric wiring.

20.

Dark Spirits

Vomit! The smell was unmistakable. This foul odor had been there for about a year. It was coming from directly in front of the dining room window. I was reminded of it every time I passed through it. It seemed to be just floating in the air. I am six feet three inches tall and it would hit me in the nose every time. It wouldn't go away, until all of a sudden, one day, it was completely gone.

I was hoping Sharon would be able to provide some sort of explanation for this but I missed my chance. I had gotten so caught up in everything that she was telling me that I completely forgot about it. But I wondered, did an animal die underneath the house? Was it weather related? And why did it suddenly go away? This led me to start to think back to the time when I first noticed it, and then to the time when I didn't notice it anymore.

I remember first smelling it right around the time when Nancy and I were completely at odds with each other. We hadn't agreed to separate yet but things were bad. We were arguing over everything. There was a lot of anger, deception, lying, manipulation, and I was feeling very depressed. I think Nancy and I both knew at that time that our short marriage would soon be over.

That summer of 2004 was ruined. I was miserable. I was emotionally drained. I hated to come home because I knew that she would be there. The packed boxes of her belongings sat in the dining room for months, piled high along the wall. And then there was this horrible smell coming from in front of the dining room window. It was very peculiar. I knew that as long as I have lived in this house, no one had ever thrown up there. I often wondered if Nancy could smell it but I never asked her. I was hoping that she was going to say something to me about it, but she never did. Maybe because at that point all communication between us had broken down. But, on the other hand, Joey never said anything about it either. Was I the only one who smelled it? I was not imagining it. I know what I smelled. I know it was sickening and I was reminded of it everyday when I passed through that part of the dining room.

Towards the end of August of that summer, Nancy had moved out. I then, became very relieved. Even though the house was an empty mess, at least there would be no more arguing, no more lies, no more sadness, no more depression and no more misery. I felt an overwhelming sense of relief. And shortly after, I was happy again. I felt excitement and was eager to move on.

It wasn't long after Nancy had left that I noticed that the smell had also left. It was no longer there. I remember standing in that very spot inhaling deep breaths and there was nothing. It was odorless.

I figured if anyone would be able to tell me anything about this, it would be Sharon. Maybe she could have shed some light on that mystery. But for now, I'll have to wait.

21.

They're Listening

Communication with one of these ghosts happened during the summer of 2005. While working on my next big construction project of gutting my son's bedroom, I had become very dependent on a battery operated clock. I had to shut down the electricity to that bedroom in fear that I would hit something while ripping out the walls and get shocked. During this time of the reconstruction I had to shut off circuits three and sixteen in my electric panel box. Shutting off these two circuits would allow me to work safely.

I kept the battery operated clock on the table in the small landing just above the stairs. This is the same table where Sharon saw the boy standing.

I constantly had to be aware of the time because I still had a schedule to follow. I was only able to work for a few hours at a time. I then had to allow time for a shower, to put on my uniform and drive to work. I paid a lot off attention to that clock during this time.

It was during one of these days when I was working on the bedroom. I picked up the clock and just kind of said out loud, "Hey, if you want to connect with me or let me know that you are here, this would be a great way to do it, through this clock."

About a half hour later, I got into the shower, got dressed and started out the backdoor to go to work. Just as I was leaving I looked up at the kitchen clock to notice that the time was 2:50 which is ten minutes late for me. I usually like to leave by 2:40 at the latest. Feeling a little anxious, I walked out of the door and went to work.

When I arrived home around midnight that evening, I went upstairs only to notice that the battery operated clock on the table had stopped ticking. It had stopped at the time 4:50, which is exactly two hours after I had walked out of the door to go to work. Thinking that this may have been a coincidence, I put the clock back down on the table and let it be.

The next morning, one of the first things I did after getting out of bed, was to walk over to the clock to see if it was working again. It wasn't. The time still said 4:50, the same as the day before.

I then went down to the kitchen, poured a glass of juice and started to talk to Agnes. I didn't say much, but I had a strong urge to say hello, so I said it.

"Hello! I know that you are here and I just wanted to tell you that you are welcome to stay here, ...oh, and I love what you did with the clock."

I then cleared the sink of dishes, put them into the dishwasher and went back upstairs. To my surprise when I got to the top of the steps I noticed that the clock was ticking again. In fact, the time now said 4:59. This means that it had been ticking for nine minutes, which was exactly the time that I was standing in the kitchen telling Agnes that I loved what she did with the clock.

22.

Ma-Ryah

I had now gotten to the point where I wanted to know who these people were, when they lived, and why they are here. I was also curious to know who was responsible for doing what in this house. And I really wanted some insight as to what the vomit smell was all about. I figured the only way that I was going to get these answers and finally get to the bottom of all of this would be to pay Sharon the fee that she charges and have her do the channeling for me to get the answers that I was looking for. Sharon was living next door now, so this would be very easy for us to do.

I called Sharon on the phone and told her that I wanted to schedule a one hour reading. I figured that this would really allow me to see first hand what channeling is and how it works.

Sharon and I agreed that the best place to do this would be at my house, in my living room. She knocked on my door at 4:30 P.M. on October 20, 2005. She sat on the worn winged back yellow chair and began setting up her tape recorder. She hooked a microphone to her shirt, unraveled her tuning forks and began to explain to me what was going to happen. She told me that Ma-Ryah comes from the seventh dimension, and that human beings are of the third dimension. The forth dimension is the astral plane which is a world just beginning to be seen and understood by our science, and that there are twelve dimensions in all.

When Ma-Ryah comes into her body, that I can ask her anything. In her world there is no guilt, embarrassment, hatred, negativity or any of those things that we experience here on earth. In her world there is only love and light. Her world can see human beings and they love them unconditionally. She also told me that Ma-Ryah's language is a bit broken and some of her grammar is not well. Her purpose for being here is not to create fear, negativity or pain, it is to promote spiritual guidance and understanding to help you overcome the pain and suffering that the human life offers, and for you to know that you are loved and cared for. There is a reason for your being here, and there are lessons to be learned. She can offer some awareness and spiritual guidance to help you through some of the more difficult times.

Sharon then asked me if I was ready. I told her that I was. She closed her eyes and sat very still in a meditating state on the yellow chair. After about forty-five seconds, a smile started to run across her face and her eyes opened. It was Sharon's body, but I was now talking to her spiritual guide from the seventh dimension, Ma-Ryah.

It seemed like Ma-Ryah was just as eager to talk about the occupants of my house as I was. The following is a transcript of the reading.

MA-RYAH: Hello, God's blessings. It is good to speak with you.

GREG: Hello Ma-Ryah.

MA-RYAH: So you would like to know a little bit about your house guests?

GREG: Yes. I would like to know very much about my house guests and maybe some other things.

MA-RYAH: Let's start with your house guests because they are very much wanting our attention.

The woman gets the name of Agnes. It is close to her name. Agnes is her middle name. We're going to tell her she can come closer. Her full name is Elizabeth Agnes Jensen, and in her time which was the late 1800's, she is already old woman. She does not like us to say old woman, but she is an older woman in the late 1800's as what would be seen as elder years in your world. She leaves this world when she is in her 78th year.

Many times people think that when a spirit shares the home with them that it is someone who is earthbound, and she (Agnes) thinks this is funny. She thinks this is funny because she went through her review and she has chosen to be around earth. She likes to be here.

She has been with you since you are 28 years of age. You have changed a lot in those years and yet in some ways you are still the same.

She is very happy to have an opportunity to be heard. She's

been waiting a long time to tell you some things. She has been wanting to talk to you.

GREG: The number 28 has always been my favorite number. That has always been *my* number. In fact, I had that as a question written on my paper. The question that I wrote was, does the number 28 hold any significance in my life?

MA-RYAH: Yes, that is when Agnes came to be with you. You will know that her first name is Elizabeth, but she's alright with Agnes.

GREG: Does she prefer Agnes to Elizabeth?

MA-RYAH: Actually, she prefers Agnes to Elizabeth and what she was called the human which was Lizzy, she did not like that. So, Agnes is alright for her.

She says that Jonathan and Sarah are a delight for her too. And Sarah is quieter. She does not let her presence be known too much. Jonathan is more active and more mischievous.

GREG: Does Jonathan play with the kitchen lights?

MA-RYAH: He plays with everything. Sarah does not do so much of that. Sarah is more of that you would be aware of movement without having sight of movement. She is more sound that you think you hear, but you are not certain you hear. She does not make much noise. She does not move things.

Jonathan though, he enjoys playing with lights, and he will move things.

GREG: How old are they?

MA-RYAH: Jonathan, as a human, when he makes transition, he is 10 years of age, and Sarah is 4 when she makes transition, (we are looking now at Sarah and Jonathan upstairs).

It is easy to think of them as children always because they appear as children, and yet they are aware, they know how long they have been out of the flesh in the linear knowledge of time, and that this is not their time frame.

GREG: So, they are brother and sister?

MA-RYAH: No, they are not. Jonathan, when he is in the flesh, he would be seen as English in his upbringing, and this area here is still under the Red Man Indian. He is one of the few English people that is here and gets the spotted fever, the measles. He dies from that.

Sarah, she is more from the 1900's period. She is 1920's and as she gets...in the lungs, the children, they bark like dogs...and their lungs...they fill up with fluid...and she is four when she makes transition.

It is the same as you in the flesh. You find one another and you have friends, and so does those in spirit. They know they are not really 4 and 10. They are no age and they are all age, but they enjoy being seen as children.

The reason that they stay in that time frame in their appearance is because though you may look at their life and say, how sad, she is only 4, her four years she was very loved. So...that is a very happy life, and so she holds to that, and the same with Jonathan. He is very much wanted and very much loved, and he very much enjoyed this world, so he chooses to stay around. You do not have anyone here that would be seen as earthbound. They are all here by choice.

GREG: Do the children visit or do they pretty much live

here?

MA-RYAH: They are here most of the time. Yes, Sarah says your house is very quiet a lot of times and that she comes down to visit with Agnes when you are not home. Otherwise, she pretty much stays upstairs.

Jonathan has been around here only about four years. Before that he was more around the water, the outside, the dunes, the woods. And Sarah, she's only been here two years of your time.

GREG: What made them come?

MA-RYAH: Agnes. Because even though they know they are not children, when they become aware of Agnes, she is like a grandmother, and so they are taken care of...the same as her father, not really to be fed and such and yet Agnes will make a lot of noise like she is cooking and for them they perceive that they are eating, but it is not the same as feeding your bodies.

GREG: Does Jonathan get upset when he does things and I don't react?

MA-RYAH: Yes, and he'll do more then, to try and get your attention.

GREG: Is he trying to tell me anything or does he do it just to play?

MA-RYAH: Just to know that he is there, and just from time to time speak out loud to him.

When your son is here, he likes your son, and your son, to ask your son when he is here, he stays here, he sleeps, that

Jonathan stands off in the far corner. The bed is here right? In the corner, Jonathan stands, and your son, he knows something is over there but he doesn't say much because he doesn't want to be seen as a little kid who maybe thinks there is a monster in the room. So he knows there is something there but he does not know for sure.

GREG: Is Jonathan mainly in the front bedroom or is he more in my son's room?

MA-RYAH: He is more in your son's room than yours. He's the one who creates the city on your wall.

GREG: That was a city?

MA-RYAH: Yes.

Sarah does not really manipulate anything in your world. She experiences in her world...here. She has toys. She has the love from Agnes, and that she perceives that if she comes down that she will walk the steps with legs like a human even though they do not have form, they have sound.

GREG: So...what I can do to Jonathan, to comfort him would be just to address it, his presence.

MA-RYAH: Yes, and when he does something to get your attention that you would correct him as if he was a physical child, you do the same with him. Let him know that it is not right, appropriate for him to do that.

For both of them to have something that is a gift for them that they may both, if they choose, move it. They may have it as theirs whether they can physically hold it or not. As energy beings, they can move it a bit.

GREG: Does Agnes get disappointed with me when I don't address her?

MA-RYAH: No, no. She's used to you not knowing she's around.

GREG: Does she have parties?

MA-RYAH: When she makes a lot of noise here, or when she creates party for herself, when she creates party for herself and the children which she does at least once a month for them, she makes noise to be heard. As in just a couple of days ago, she made much noise, and so she hopes you heard her.

GREG: What would I hear?

MA-RYAH: You will hear the sounds as someone is in the kitchen. She is able to make the sounds of a cabinet open and close. She is able to make the sound of pans to be moved. She is able to make the utensils sound as if they are being touched, and she is able to make the sound of feet walking.

GREG: Has she ever made any of these sounds and has seen me turn to look?

MA-RYAH: Yes! Yes, she has. She definitely has.

And sometimes she will stand when you are cooking. She's not used to, until she sees you, except for when like there was someone hired to do cooking, she was not used to seeing man cook. So when she first starts to be around you now as you are, she stands very close behind you when you are cooking. So you may turn when you get that feeling over the shoulder that she's standing right there watching you cooking.

GREG: Does she want me to know that she's there?

MA-RYAH: Yes, she does. Does she get upset if you don't? No.

GREG: Is it hard for her to present herself? Does it take or use up a lot of her energy to present herself in a human form for me to see?

MA-RYAH: For you to see? No, because she is there in spirit, not in a long linear time and she is past her review. She's able to manifest not a full denseness enough to be seen, and if you desire, she will work with you for you to be able to see her.

This is very much like the vessel who was speaking to you before. For you to sit and to thank her for helping you. That is one thing as humans you are taught, ask and you shall receive. And yet, whatever you ask is already known that you are going to ask for it. But instead, if you ask in a very subtle way for the human, the ego, it sets up the opportunity for you not to receive and you get tired of asking or you think that you're not being listened to or that you are not loved or cared about by spirit, by God. So just thank her that (she just got bigger, brighter) just thank her that she works with you so you're able to see her. And it is easier to begin to see by not direct looking. We are able to see by direct looking. We see them through the vessels eyes. We do not lose the spirit because we do not have fear, because we would be afraid of self. She is most comfortable in the kitchen and the table area.

GREG: Does she turn on that light? (Pointing to the tall touch lamp on the long sideboard table in the dining room).

82

MA-RYAH: Yes, she does. But most of the time it is Jonathan doing it.

When you desire to see her, you're able to sit in either of the chairs and she will sit in the chair to the left of you. So that if you sit in this chair here, (pointing to chair) you look straight ahead and just relax your eyes. So your eyes are like when you are day dreaming. They are opened, you are seeing, but you are not focused on any point specifically. So you look that way, and as your peripheral relaxes, you will begin to see first like the heat waves of a road. You will see movement of energy. Then you will see little sparks of light, then it zooms up like when you watch a fire–an outside fire, and how the sparks fly up and they are like tadpoles almost. That is how you will see her light first. And then in time, those tadpoles will begin to collect and you will have awareness of a light. And once you have awareness of a light, you are then able to turn more to see more direct with your eyes recognizing that your initial sight, you will be shocked, and allow that to be alright if you lose sight of her. You relax, allow the peripheral to pick her up again. And then in time you will be able to see her and hold the sight of her without losing it.

GREG: Now is that the same with Jonathan and Sarah?

MA-RYAH: Yes, the same.

GREG: They're willing?

MA-RYAH: Yes. Jonathan's very willing. Sarah is a little shy and yet she is willing if Jonathan will be with her.

GREG: Are the children wondering why there is no woman here?

MA-RYAH: No, because Agnes is here. So for them, a woman *is* here. And in the time frame that both of them lived in, it was not uncommon for a woman not to be around. For she would become ill, or she would die giving birth. So they are used to not always having a mother. The type of woman around were grandmothers, aunts...they are used to that.

GREG: A couple of weeks ago I was going to Ocean City and I invited the children to come in the car with me. I was wondering if they came.

MA-RYAH: No, they did not. They do not understand what a car is. So, if you desire (they are both peeking through the railing, Jonathan and Sarah behind him. So...they are here very much listening).   So, if you desire them to go somewhere with you to experience and to see, especially Jonathan because the area is very different than the world he existed in, explain to them what a car is and what its purpose is, the sounds that it makes and how it accomplishes what it does. Remember, Jonathan was at the time of mainly human legs that were walking to travel from one point to the next.

Sarah, there were some cars in your world at that time, but not many and mostly what she would see humans travel in was horse and wagon, and buggies. So teach them about your car.

GREG: Do either of them touch me?

MA-RYAH: Sarah does, and she touches you a lot on your hand. And she touches you right here on your face. When you are sleeping, it is more Sarah that is around you than it is Jonathan.

GREG: She just watches me?

MA-RYAH: Yes...yes.

If you are able to see her and indeed you shall at one point, you will see she is very beautiful child, and she dresses in the period of the 1920's just as a child that age would dress.

Jonathan is more basic in his dress. He's more a coursed shirt and he is the short pants below his knee and yet not all the way down for he is not man yet, and...bare feet.

While Sarah has her leg stocking overings, and her shoes that are buckled, and she has bows, big bows in her hair, and she dresses as she was dressed.

GREG: Is there something wrong with Jonathan's legs?

MA-RYAH: He has a lot of problems with his thighs on both legs. As the human being before, he has the death of the measles. Because he is in an accident with an ax in helping to cut the tree, he cuts across. He does not sever his legs, but he cuts so that the muscle is weak and then he gets the spotted fever and then he dies before his legs are fully healed.

So his legs in time would have healed and because they have not, he carries that weakness. He does not really have to carry a weakness.

GREG: But they are both very comfortable with me?

MA-RYAH: Yes, they are.

GREG: ...and living here?

MA-RYAH: Yes. Jonathan is very much enthralled with your son because his life is very different than Jonathan's was, and now they are aware that this is not their time frame. They still only have the knowledge of their time frame because they hold to the persona of who they were even though they know they are not.

When you are able to see them, they are able to tell you a lot about what it is like for them as children in that time frame. Agnes says don't get Jonathan started, he'll make a lot of talk.

Sometimes when you are in the twilight sleep, you're not yet asleep, but yet you are no longer awake, that is easy time for them to talk, for you to hear them. The challenge for you will be to be able to stay in that twilight and not jerk out of it.

So if you would like they will start to speak to you. Sarah will speak to you since she stays with you while you sleep, and she will start to speak. So, in the twilight when you hear them, talk to yourself ahead of time and give yourself permission to hear them and stay in that twilight and forgive yourself if you do not stay in it.

It is the same as when you are teaching your son when he is learning the music. Each time you learn a little bit more, and you accomplish a bit more.

GREG: Have I passed through Jonathan on the staircase?

MA-RYAH: Yes, you have.

GREG: Many times?

MA-RYAH: Yes, many times.

And for them it is, you as humans, you sometimes can feel it. You just walk through somebody. For them it is...um...not assault, is not the right word. It is movement for them.

When you are walking up, to just say I know you can see me. I don't see you yet, so they can step out of your way. Let them know that you really don't want to step through them.

Most humans do not even give thought to the spirit as they walk through.

GREG: I imagine I walk through Agnes...

MA-RYAH: Agnes a lot, but she puts herself in that place so you do not have to be worried when you walk through her. She does not mind it.

GREG: Does Agnes go into the refrigerator. I thought I saw something walk into the refrigerator one night.

MA-RYAH: She doesn't ever go in the refrigerator. She knows that you keep food there and she sees food going. She sees food come out, but she has no use for it even in her cooking for Jonathan and Sarah.

When you start to become aware of energy, it is not only spirit. You become aware of...you become aware of the energy that is all things, everything in your world. You are able to, with your science, to have the knowledge that have as a solid and yet it happens so rapidly in your world that it appears to be solid and yet it is not. It is made of molecules and the molecules are always in motion. And sometimes with your camera you are able to catch what is solid appearing as unsolid because you happen to capture the molecules in that rapid transition that they are always in.

GREG: I need to ask you about a terrible smell that was in my dining room. It was the smell of vomit. It was horrible and was coming from in front of the dining room window. It was there for about a year, and then one day it just went away. Is there anything you can tell me about that?

MA-RYAH: When you have a smell like that, when it is

like vomit, or when sulfur, when it is like fermented meat or vegetation, there is then an energy that is around. That even in spirit only knows itself through fear. So when that occurs you are able to cleanse that area by using either your spirit beliefs as in a prayer, or for it to be attended to by others–to be told to leave.

The vessel (Sharon) smokes her house and she is able to use sage and you are able to use cedar. In your area here, cedar is stronger because that was the sacred scent of the indigenous people.

Some prefer sage rather than cedar but which ever you use, the qualities of those plants and because they are most often used in sacred ceremonies, whether indigenous or modern, people still use them now. They are the same as in your churches, the incense is used. It cleans the air. It raises the vibration.

GREG: Just so I understand you correctly, it was a dark spirit? I had a dark spirit in my dining room?

MA-RYAH: What you would see as dark, yes.

GREG: ...and it just...what... hung out there?

MA-RYAH: Yes.

GREG: In the same spot?

MA-RYAH: Yes. Many times when you are unhappy as human beings, you will draw to some spirits as what you would see as dark, as in fear, demons. We do not ever see them that way because we see only an energy that has forgotten it is love.

If you react to them in fear, that is their nourishment. If you

88

are able to be centered in love and send love to them, they then chose of their own choice not to stay because they have chosen to know themselves not as love.

Now you have knowledge of us, and we speak of ourselves as, "us" or "we" because we are the spirit and all the sole together. So it is not a singular like, "I." We are aware of ourselves in connection to all aspects of, "us" in our world and all in our world speak in that way.

GREG: Yes, at that time, I was miserable. My wife and I were separating and this was a very unhappy place. There was a lot of bitterness, anger and depression.

MA-RYAH: Yes, you are always able to call on, "us" and we will help them leave. We take them to either a place of love so they can experience what that love is and to remember. And, if they still choose not to be part of love, then we take them to what your world calls the astral plane, where they may perceive themselves as they knew themselves. Then...from time to time they will be approached by other beings of love to remind them that they have free will to choose. All spirit has free will.

When they are of fear, you are easily able to discern through smell, through feeling. You may walk into a part of a room and it does not feel right. Trust what you feel. Fill it with the sacred, fill it with love and it will leave. If you fill it with fear, they stay and become stronger.

GREG: Fear is food for them?

MA-RYAH: Yes, yes.

You may want to leave a gift for Jonathan and Sarah. Something they could have for their own. One thing Sarah has always wanted but never had was a rag doll.

89

GREG: Okay, where would I put it?

MA-RYAH: You can put it in the corner of your room.

And Jonathan, if you desire for him to learn about the car, you could get him a small car so he could see. You can put them either in your son's room or at the top of the stairs.

GREG: Okay.

MA-RYAH: Are you content?

GREG: Yes.

MA-RYAH: We must balance out the vessel.

With that, all talking stopped, there was silence in the room and after thirty seconds to a minute, Ma-Ryah was gone, the vessel opened her eyes and it was Sharon again.

Sharon and I talked some more. We talked about my reading and about channeling in general. She then handed me the recorded tape, I paid her, and then she went home.

23.

The Significance of Twenty-Eight

Elizabeth Agnes Jensen. This is the woman living with me. That means that both psychics were right. Monique from the coffee shop told me that she was getting a very strong, "E" to her name and Sharon in the yard had told me that her name was Agnes. Monique was speaking of her first name and Sharon was speaking of her middle name. They both had the same person but were giving different names for that person.

I suppose I was disappointed to hear that the children are not here because of me. They are only here because of Agnes. They found Agnes and came to be with her. Agnes however, is here for me. For what reason? I don't know. I only know that she wants to tell me some things. But why would she want to come to me in the first place? She has been with me since I was twenty-eight years old. I am forty-one now. That means that she has been with me for thirteen years. And, if it weren't for Jonathan playing around with everything, there is a good chance that I would have never known it. How would I have?

Oddly enough, the number twenty-eight has been the predominant number in my life. Over the years that number just seemed to work for me. It just kept popping up in enough places for me to take notice. I always called it my lucky number or my favorite number. Now I learn that it was when I was twenty-eight years old that Agnes came to be with me.

I strongly believe now that Jonathan was desperately

trying to get my attention. He very much wanted me to know that he was there. His playing with the lights was endless. I would go into the kitchen, the overhead light would go out. Now I believe that he was with me many times just there watching me almost as if he were waving a big flag saying, "I'm here, I'm right here!"

My son Joey was very much afraid of that corner of the bedroom that Ma-Ryah was talking about. There was a heating vent in the floor that he kept asking me to cover up because he was afraid something was going to come out of it. This side of the room was definitely a worry for him and he seldom went over there. And now, of course, we find out that in that corner of the room was where Jonathan would stand and watch Joey sleep.

24.

Rag Dolls and Matchbox Cars

I wanted to get their gifts. This somehow made sense to me, to get them something, something of their own that they could manipulate if they wanted to. It would be theirs only. Within the next few days, I went to a few antique stores looking for an old rag doll. Not only did I find one, but I found three. I bought them all. I set up a stool in the corner of my bedroom over the vent and placed the dolls on it. Today, this is where those dolls sit.

Joey offered to give Jonathan some of his older matchbox cars. He said Jonathan could have them. He set five of them all lined up at the top of the landing in the hallway above the stairs. Joey also took some of his plastic green army men, and his cowboys and Indians that sat on horses, and also set them up around the cars. There are thirty-eight pieces in all. This includes twenty-three cowboys, Indians and green army men, ten horses and five matchbox cars. He and I have agreed that neither one of us will touch them. We agreed to just let them be and to see what happens.

They have been set up for three months. He set them up so that the cars would all be in a straight line. The horses and men he just set up randomly within the area under the table. I always notice Jonathan's toys because they are at the top of the stairs on the landing. I can't walk by without noticing them. At least twice a day, either going up the stairs or coming down the stairs, I have to pass them.

Do they move? Yes, they do. He has moved them on at least six different occasions within that three month time frame. And in addition to that, I will find pieces that have been knocked over.

The most shocking time was when Joey and I were walking up the stairs one evening. I was in front and he was right behind me. Suddenly, I stopped in my tracks at the top of the landing only to look down to notice that all of the thirty-eight pieces had moved closer together. They were now a much tighter group.

During other times, only the figures on the left side had moved, or one of the cars became completely unaligned with the others. There was one time in particular when I was focusing on two pieces only. It was the red matchbox fire truck and a green soldier that was down on one knee firing his rifle. These two pieces were on the end to the left so it was easy to keep an eye on them. After the course of about two weeks, I was shocked to see that it was those two pieces that had moved. The fire truck was now two inches further away from the rest of the cars and the soldier firing the rifle was now shooting in the opposite direction.

The most interesting aspect about this for me was that Jonathan knew that these were the two pieces that I was focusing on at the time. He was able to read that energy, which spirits are able to do. He manipulated the objects that he knew I would notice.

I honestly don't know if Sarah manipulates the dolls. I know that they are still on the stool and my guess would be that they have never left the stool. They are basically still set up just the way I set them up, only they have slipped down a bit. I don't know whether to attribute that to Sarah touching them or it's just a slippery stool.

According to Ma-Ryah though, Sarah doesn't do much of the things that Jonathan does, and that she is able to play with the dolls without physically holding them or touching them.

25.

Ghosts and Spirits

I have been wrong in calling the occupants of my house "ghosts." They are not ghosts. They are spirits. And, there is clearly a difference. The occupants of my house are spirits who have crossed over to another dimension and have decided to come back because they want to be here. They chose to be here. They are enjoying spending time in this world.

Ghosts, on the other hand, are stuck here until some other spirit leads them, or helps them to move on or to cross over. They live in a lower frequency than spirits, and are having a difficult time leaving the life that they just had. Most ghosts are unhappy, afraid, unsettled, and some can be down right angry. Most ghosts are very much lost, but once they are found and guided, they are happy to be returned to love.

I asked Ma-Ryah to explain what exactly a ghost is. I wanted this clarification so I would know exactly what my visitors were. She explained it this way.

"The being of ghost is one who is still afraid to let go of the life they have just left for many reasons, but sometimes your world sees it as they are not yet finished. They are not complete in what they have been doing and therefore they hang around in order to have it completed. Sometimes that is truth. There is something left undone that is to complete what they are there for, or what was set in motion is only able to be completed while in the flesh.

Sometimes it is because they are very afraid of what

is beyond that according to what they have been taught in the human world. And much of what is taught in the name of God in your world is fear based. And so humans can be afraid to return to all that is, for what is going to happen to them, which is only love, and yet that belief is able to be held so strong that they will not let go of it.

Many ghosts in that way will spend thousands of linear years recycling that belief, adding to it, and building to it. And the more that the layers are built to them, the more you have the ability for the smells, the physical manifestations, the narrowing in of the human fear and magnifying it to the human."

World renowned psychic Sylvia Browne explains the difference between a ghost and a spirit using the analogy of an electric fan. She says to picture the fan in the "off" position. When the fan is off you can clearly see that the fan has three blades. When you turn the fan on low, you can still see the blades but not as clearly. You know that the blades are there, but you cannot distinctively pick out each blade individually. This is the ghost.

However, when you turn the fan on high, you know the blades are there but you can't see them. You see right through them. But just because you can't see the blades doesn't mean that the blades aren't there. They are there. This would be the spirit.

There are some very telling clues if spirits are visiting. Some things to take notice of could include anything of an electrical nature such as doorbells ringing with no one there, clocks stopping and then starting again on their own, televisions going on or channels changing on their own, telephones ringing, or washers, dryers, and kitchen appliances working on their own.

They will also play music boxes, take keys, and will leave coins in strange places. They will move photographs of themselves, or will move other objects that they know you will take notice of. They can also leave an indentation on a bed or couch indicating that they had been sitting there.

They are trying to get your attention for no other reason than for you to simply acknowledge that they are there.

26.

She Was Drawn to You

A lot had been answered about what was going on in this house, but I still had many questions. And, the question that was most on my mind was, why did Agnes come to be with me in the first place? She has been with me for thirteen years. Why did she come? For what reason? And, why me? Why not someone else? What is this all about? I know that she wants me to slow down but slow down with what? What does she mean by that?

For this answer I knew that I was going to have to go back to Sharon. I had this plus two more questions that I really wanted answered. I figured if I could get these answers then I could finally put the pieces of this mysterious puzzle together.

At this point, the three questions that weighed heaviest on my mind were,

1. Agnes has been with me since I was twenty-eight. Why?

2. Did Agnes, Jonathan and Sarah ever know each other as human beings here on earth?

3. There will be times when I have a lot of activity in the house, and then there will be periods of nothing. This nothing could go on for months at a time. Is there a reason for that?

I called Sharon on the phone to set up an appointment to come see her. It was after Christmas but before the new year. It was a few days before the year 2006.

Sharon was now living in Cape May, and I offered to come to her house instead of her having to drive all the way to mine.

I pulled into her driveway. She was outside waiting to greet me with her dog Angel. We talked briefly and then we went in. She took me on a little tour of her place until we finally settled in the living room. I sat down on the sectional sofa and she sat down across from me.

For close to twenty minutes, we simply talked. We talked as friends. She told me some of the things that were going on with her and her sister Lou Ann. And we just talked about things in general. The conversation was comfortable and relaxing and I was glad that we were able to do that.

After about twenty minutes, she was ready to call in Ma-Ryah. I was ready. Sharon closed her eyes, put herself into her meditative state and after about forty-five seconds her eyes opened and it was now Ma-Ryah speaking through Sharon's body.

MA-RYAH: God's blessings. It's good to see you again.

GREG: Hello Ma-Ryah. It's good to speak with you again also. I have a question that has been on my mind for some time. I am very curious to know.

MA-RYAH: Yes.

GREG: It is about Agnes, the older woman living with me.

MA-RYAH: Yes.

GREG: I am 41 years old now. Agnes has been with me since I was 28 years old. That is 13 years my time. What is it that brought her to me in the first place? Why Me? For what reason?

MA-RYAH: Because...because you are very similar to what she is when she is a human being. It is how you are with allowing others to come into your life to be loving. She was very much the same way. She desired to have someone in her life and to be in a relationship of love and yet when it came, her fear of it ending was so great that she would not allow it to remain. And so at the same time, as when the human self is, all I desire in life is to have love, they are the words saying that, yet in the moments of creating experiences with the one to love, she was pushing and creating distance and creating opportunities to not have the love remain. So when you are 28, you are creating very strongly in that way. So, she is drawn to you so that you are able to receive wisdom that she now has from being on the other side.

GREG: Is she trying to protect me to make sure that this doesn't happen to me?

MA-RYAH: Yes. Trying is not accurate because that is human term, and yet she is communicating being around you to send you energy, to send you thought. To help you be aware that here is pattern, here is what you do, so that when an opportunity arises for you to have what you desire, you will be aware of the very subtle ways that you destroy that.

GREG: Is that a regret in her life?

MA-RYAH: Very much so. She remained with a husband that she wed and yet they were not together. And through her later years of her life was very much without love, without companionship. She was very much isolated in herself.

Then, when she had her review, when she leaves the physical, she sees very clearly, here is where she pushed that

100

love away. And so the husband, out of defense of his heart and fear for his heart created a barrier that he would not allow her to get through. So they both created the same thing. And then, just like the same side of a magnet, same to same will repel. This is what happens. And so with regret from the human self, she thought here was what she desired and she did not see it.

GREG: So this is all about relationships. This whole thing is about my failing relationships with women and how she doesn't want me to make the same mistakes that she made.

MA-RYAH: Yes.

GREG: She saw that I was wrong in what I was creating and she came here to help me.

MA-RYAH: Yes.

GREG: Agnes made her transition in her 78th year. Can you give me that year, in which she makes her transition?

MA-RYAH: Yes, she made transition in the year 1898.

GREG: Was she living in the United States at that time?

MA-RYAH: Yes, in the area of what is Chicago of your world.

GREG: Did she have any children of her own?

MA-RYAH: She had son and his name was Edward.

GREG: Did Agnes, Jonathan and Sarah ever know each other as human beings in this world, or have they simply only known each other in the spirit world?

MA-RYAH: Only in spirit. They come together as old friends. Because when you are in spirit once, you are returned to spirit, and you let go of the human self, and that takes time in the linear understanding. Then, you are drawn back to what is seen as family, and you reconnect, each able to create separate and yet to come together at thought.

GREG: So they all came together and gathered in a place which happens to be my house?

MA-RYAH: Yes.

GREG: Will more spirits be coming to join them?

MA-RYAH: From time to time, but not so many will stay. You may occasionally have one that seems to settle in for a few months or a year, but in spirit, that is nothing. But in your term, you will find a couple of months visit to a year...sometimes a little more.

GREG: Do Jonathan and Sarah like the gifts that my son and I left for them? Is there anything else that they desire?

MA-RYAH: No. They are very content with what you have left them...very content.

Were you aware two nights ago when Sarah came down to look at your fish?

GREG: No.

MA-RYAH: She came down and was looking at the fish and she thought maybe you heard her because she moved some of the stuff on your table a little bit.

GREG: Was I in the room at the time?

MA-RYAH: Yes.

GREG: That brings me to my next question. It seems that there will be times when I have all of this stuff going on and then there is a period when there will be nothing. Some of those periods could be months. Is there a reason for that?

MA-RYAH: When there is that nothing occurring, sometimes it is that they are not in the house at the moment, and other times it is that they are occupied in other ways, and other times it is that they have given up that you are paying attention to them.

GREG: If they are not in the house at the time, then where do they go ?

MA-RYAH: Because Jonathan and Sarah are seen as children, they will go very often to children. And so while they are not in your house, especially Jonathan is more as um...a guide for children that are making from physical to spirit–that transition. So when there is a child that he is drawn to, he then will leave your home and he will be who he really is, which is a transition guide.

Sarah does not do that. When she leaves your home she is going to places of your world and going to places in spirit. She is still very much...if she were able to be physical, she would have one foot in physical and one foot in spirit. And since she is full spirit now, she still yet remains around your earth and learns of your earth as what would be seen as preparation for when she in the linear time reenters the flesh.

GREG: When it comes my day for me to make transition, do you think that they will be with me?

MA-RYAH: Yes.

GREG: All three of them?

MA-RYAH: Yes

27.

Lessons to Be Learned

The fact of the matter is, I have been married twice and divorced twice. In between the marriages, I became engaged to another woman and that also failed. I have one child from my first marriage named Joseph.

My first marriage was to Beverly and it lasted only two years. It was at this time of my life that I was twenty-eight years old.

Three years after the final divorce from Beverly, I became engaged to someone that I worked with. We bought a house together. In this relationship however, we were both wanting more but not getting it from each other. We cancelled the wedding which was to occur in seven months and sold the house.

Nancy was my second wife. We married only after a year and a half of knowing each other. This marriage ended after eighteen months.

Agnes knew that there had been three significant women in my life. She also commented that she liked the first one better than the last one. "The last one was harsh with her words," she told Ma-Ryah. Nothing was said about the woman in the middle.

Agnes came to be with me when I was twenty-eight because she knew then that I was starting to create something that shouldn't be created. Something that I would repeat time and time again with whoever I was involved in a relationship with. And, because Agnes was the same way in her life, this was why she was drawn to me. She did not want me to make the same mistakes and have the same regrets as her.

There are many more things that came out in the readings that I haven't discussed in this book. Things that I will hold very dear to me. But I know now, that Agnes is with me. I know which dreams are sent from her for me to look more closely, and I know when she is trying to tell me something.

And when the next relationship comes around, it is her that will be keeping a close eye on it to see if I am applying the lessons that I have learned. If I have become more aware of what needs to be different, and am I willing to change it. It will require more risk and more vulnerability, but the rewards could result in a deeper love, a love that I have never experienced before, a love that I never thought possible. This is what she would like to see created. And once it is created, to not push it away because of fear. Fear of someone getting too close, fear of losing someone again, fear of letting myself go.

At least now, I have a chance to correct my mistakes and to learn from them. After all, life is a school, and we are all here to learn. Each and every one of us is weak in some area of our lives. It is in those areas that we are here to learn and to improve on. During this life, for me, that area is relationships.

I am grateful that Agnes was drawn to me because now I have a new beginning with a new perspective. And if it weren't for Jonathan creating havoc around here, there is a good chance that I would have never gone to see Monique in the coffee shop, or to be led right to Sharon which seemed to just fall right on my lap. The time had come for me to listen. Agnes knew that my ears were open and that I was ready to listen. Everything happens for a reason. One may not know it for years to come, but there is a purpose for everything that happens.

28.

Different Worlds/Old Friends

In my quest for answers, I now realize that these three spirits were not in this house when I bought it five years ago. They have no connection to this one hundred year old house at all. It had nothing to do with the three funerals that were held here or the two year old girl who died upstairs in the bedroom.

It is about a spirit in the spirit world who was drawn to a certain human being on earth. This spirit has been following this human being for thirteen years trying to send energy to that person. Energy that would help them see what it is that they are doing wrong in their relationships and to help lead them in a new direction, to try a different way.

The spirits name is Elizabeth Agnes Jensen. She was born in 1820 and died in 1898. She was seventy-eight years old. She lived in the area of what we know as Chicago, was married and had one son. The last years of her life were lonely ones because of the walls that she created in her relationship with her husband. She can now see, after being on the other side, that it was her that pushed the love away instead of trying to bring it closer. She sees a human being making the same mistakes that she did and that is why she is drawn to him. That human being is me.

I have moved four times since I was twenty-eight years old and Agnes has found me each time.

Jonathan was born in 1841 and died when he was ten years old from the measles. He had wounds on his legs which never completely healed while he accidentally cut himself with an ax while helping to cut down a tree. The combination of the measles and the wounds to his legs caused him to make transition at his young age.

Sarah lived in the 1920's and died from too much fluid in her lungs. She was four years old, and is still dressed in the period of the 1920's. She was a shy withdrawn child who loved music, flowers and dolls.

Both Jonathan and Sarah were drawn to my house because of Agnes. Jonathan came around the year 2001 and Sarah around 2003. They found Agnes who was a long time friend in spirit. Jonathan, Sarah and Agnes never knew each other as human beings, as they were of different time frames. They just happened to meet up again as old friends in spirit and joined together in my house.

Jonathan very much wanted his presence to be known by my son and I. He wanted us to know that he was there. He was the one getting his hands into everything, playing and experimenting with things. These were the things that became very noticeable to my son and I as we were the ones on the human side wondering what in the world was going on.

Now that my investigation to the on goings of this house is coming to an end for now, I realized that I no longer lose electrical power to the house. I no longer have to reset clocks or change the message on the answering machine. The jokes played with things appearing and disappearing has also stopped. We know that Jonathan is here and that is all that he wanted in the first place. All this time, he just wanted to get our attention. And now that he has it, he no longer has to make the huge effort in trying to achieve it.

Jonathan will still say hello through the lights by turning them on and off when he is here, and I will always follow the advice of Ma-Ryah and call out to him. I will say, "Hello Jonathan, glad you're here, it's always good to have you." I want to make sure that he doesn't feel ignored and want to reassure him that he is indeed welcome to stay.

Joey loves it when Jonathan is here. Both Joey and Jonathan are the same age. They are both ten years old. Joey finds the whole idea of Jonathan really "cool" and he has given Jonathan complete permission to play with any of his toys.

We also have a picture of Jonathan on the staircase which was taken with a digital camera. Over a Thanksgiving weekend, Joey and his two cousins Abigail and Alec were putting on a show in front of the stairs. They were singing songs, laughing and having fun. Pictures were taken and the appearance of a white "orb" showed up on many of the pictures at different spots on the stairs. Jonathan's energy was captured on film. He apparently had come down to watch the show also. Sarah was not in the picture.

Agnes continues to send me messages through thought. She helps me find things, and she touches me every once in a while on my neck or shoulder.

I have a strong desire to communicate with Agnes without a medium. But as Ma-Ryah explains it, we are now from two different worlds. Agnes is going to have to slow down her vibrational frequency and I am going to have to practice remembering through meditation what it was like to be in spirit. With time and practice however, the two worlds will eventually come together and communication will be possible through writing. Agnes has a desire to write a book of poems with me. Something that she would be able to look at from time to time with her name on it.

29.

Love or Fear

I suppose I feel blessed to have such an extraordinary experience such as this happen to me. This wasn't something that I went looking for or had asked for. It all came to me and simply fell on my lap. I never saw it as a frightening experience. I saw it more as just an unbelievable one.

I was not born with any kind of psychic ability. I can't see, hear or communicate with the dead, and up until now I had no desire to do so. It is my understanding though that all human beings are a little bit psychic. We know when something feels right and when it doesn't. We may meet someone and in an instant know that we don't want to have anything to do with that person. We also may walk into a house or a room, and get a very uncomfortable feeling being there. We tend to call this our intuition. And, we have all had experiences happen to us which we so commonly call, "coincidences."

Some people are born with the natural psychic "gift." For others, it is like a muscle that we don't know how to use. It has to be practiced and developed. For most people, it would be like sitting down at a piano for the first time and expecting to play a sonata or a concerto. It isn't going to happen. One must hear the instrument, learn the instrument, develop an ear for it, and develop an eye for reading the notes.

For now, for anyone to improve their own psychic ability, the first thing that they can do is to listen. Listen to their intuition and to trust it. And, to pay attention to your dreams. It is the easiest way for a spirit to get in touch with you. They will speak to you through your dreams because they know that all of your filters are down and that you are listening. These dreams will appear very real to you and you will remember them. Even after you have woken you will remember them quite vividly.

If you are someone who has dreamt of a friend or loved one who has passed and you woke up with the feeling that you were talking to them, and that they were there with you, don't be quick to dismiss it as, only a dream. It is possible that that spirit was actually talking to you. They came for a visit.

According to Ma-Ryah, the greatest problem with human beings is that they just don't listen. They would rather listen to anything else, or to have any other explanation rather than the spirit world.

Each and every one of us is guided by spirit. There are spirits all around us everyday on this planet, as well as ghosts who are still stuck in our dimension. Whatever the case, there is so much going on around us that we never hear or see, but that doesn't mean that it is not there.

Also, as mentioned before, we are all here to learn. Life is a school. We are here to learn who we are and who we are not.

Living as a human being on earth is a very difficult life to live, but find it comforting to know that there are spirits guiding us through the journey. They won't make the decisions for you, but they will nudge you to go one way or the other. Whether you live in love or fear, those spirits are with you, they love you and they are there for you. Listen to them and communicate with them. They can hear you. And if you can accept that into your life, then there will never be a day when you are ever truly alone. What your eyes can see is only half of what there is.

AFTERWARDS

Coincidences
Guided By Spirit Examples
Making the Connection

It has been said that there are no coincidences. Here are some examples of things that have happened to me, as I'm sure you have your own stories. You be the judge.

Is it a coincidence?

On the morning of September 15, 2005, as I started to back out of the driveway to leave for work, I suddenly had a very strong urge to know where my hazard lights were. I felt around the dashboard and located them. I tested them to make sure that they worked and then continued on backing out of the driveway and drove to work.

While driving home in the afternoon, that same day, my car broke down on the busy highway. The car seized up as smoke was erupting from my engine. Apparently, the service station that worked on the car the day before had never put the radiator cap back on the radiator. Fortunately, I was able to locate my hazard lights in a hurry as the cars were speeding by.

Is it a coincidence?

I hadn't heard from my son in two days. It was starting to weigh heavily on my mind. I was standing in the kitchen thinking about him and was starting to worry about him, hoping that everything was alright. Suddenly, the phone rings. It was him calling, just wanting to say, "Hi."

Is it a coincidence?

The night before I met Sharon in the backyard, my son had brought home a borrowed CD of AC/DC live. On the cover and on the inside jacket was a picture of lead guitarist Angus Young. That's an odd name I thought to myself. I spent a good amount of time looking at the pictures and focusing on the names of the players in the band. I focused on his name in particular because I thought that it was such a peculiar name.

It was the next day when I met Sharon, the channeler from New York in the yard for the first time. It was then that she told me that the woman living with me goes by, not Angus, but Agnes.

Is it a coincidence?

After searching the classified adds for weeks in the newspaper for a used drum set to buy my son, I had decided to give up. Everything that was listed in the paper at that time was well over $1,000. I only wanted to spend $500 at the most. After saying a few prayers in asking for help, I discovered within a few days an old friend of mine had stopped by to tell me that his wife was going to have a baby soon, and that he was going to sell some of his band equipment for some extra money. His five piece black Tama drum set with Zildjian cymbals was one of the items for sale. Did I know anybody that would want to buy them? He was hoping to get $500 for them.

Is it a coincidence?

After a half hour of searching the house, garage and shed for two missing microphones for my recorder, I went down to the basement one last time. Even though I was unsuccessful in finding the microphones, I did take notice to an old piece of furniture from the 1940's that I had down there. It was an old pie safe. I suddenly forgot about the microphones for the moment and started thinking about where I could fit this great piece of furniture upstairs. Where could I put it? I looked at it, and found it in great condition. I then opened it up to see what it looked like inside, for it had been a long time. Inside of it were the microphones.

Is it a coincidence?

When Joey was five years old I took him to the rides at an amusement park. There was one ride in particular that I tried feverishly to get him to go on. On this ride, you sit in a car and go along a track up and down hills. It was similar to a slow moving roller coaster. He refused. He absolutely refused to go on it. I tried to convince him that it would be okay and that it was safe. "No, Daddy, no!" he cried. I remember him saying that he didn't like the way it looked, and that's why he didn't want to go on it.

Two weeks later a mother and daughter were killed at that amusement park. They were thrown out of a car after the breaks failed on one of the rides. The car apparently rolled backwards and slammed into the car behind it throwing the mother and daughter out of the car and onto the ground. The ride in which they were killed was the ride that my son absolutely refused to go on.

Is it a coincidence?

While digging through some old papers, I found a recipe that an old friend had given me. I hadn't seen that recipe or that friend in close to four years. Knowing that I hadn't cooked it in a long time, I bought the ingredients and made it that night for dinner.

The next afternoon, at a McDonald's restaurant, I bumped into the old friend. Our cars were parked next to each other in the parking lot.

Is it a coincidence?

It was New Year's Eve, the night before the year 2006. I bought a bottle of champagne around 7:00 P.M. to get the party started. I popped it open and pulled one of the champagne glasses from my glass rack. Before pouring, I noticed that the glass that I had pulled off of the rack was one of my late grandmother's champagne glasses. She had been dead for twenty-six years. I filled the glass with champagne, picked it up and spoke out, "Happy New Year Grandmom, and thanks for the glasses."

Just then one of the light bulbs in the track lighting blew, making a loud pop, and the light went out.

JOEY

After sharing my experiences, the question that I am most often asked is, "How was your son with all of this? Was he okay during all of this, and is he okay now?"

The truth of the matter is that Joey was always the calm one. I was the one that was a mess. He thought that it was cool that we had ghosts and he loved telling the stories to others. He would only get upset when he saw me upset. "Are you alright Dad?" He would always ask. I was always much more disturbed by what was going on than he was.

There were those times of course, when he didn't want to go upstairs by himself at night, and very often he would climb into bed with me, and...oh yes, the corner of the room with the vent. That was a problem for a while.

However, at the same time, a lot of quality time was spent together. Joey and I spent a lot of time talking, playing, hanging out, and just trying to sort this whole thing out together.

Later, it became very exciting for Joey especially around the time that he found out that the spirit of Jonathan is a ten year old boy, which was the same age as him. That became very comforting to him. It was also very comforting for Joey to find out that Jonathan is completely enthralled with Joey's way of life and in the toys that he is able to play with.

Joey loves it when Jonathan is here and is disappointed when he isn't. Once you've gotten to know Jonathan the way that we have, Jonathan can be very much missed.

For questions or comments, write:

gygregory@aol.com

or

"Ghosts"
P.O. Box 153
Somers Point, NJ 08244

For other books by Gregory Young, please visit:

www.JettyBooks.com